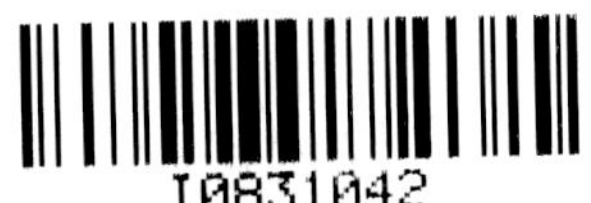

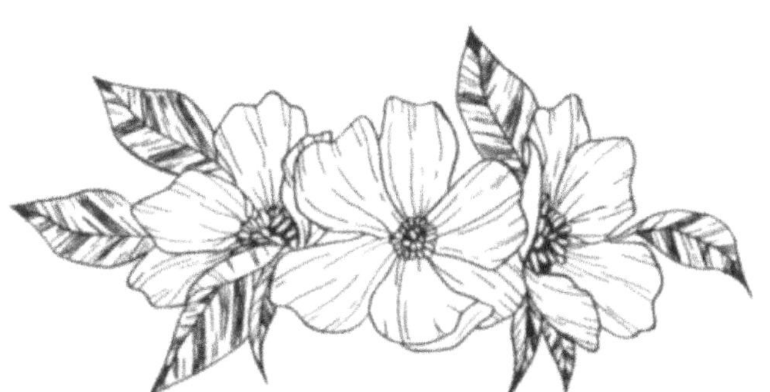

This book belongs to

....

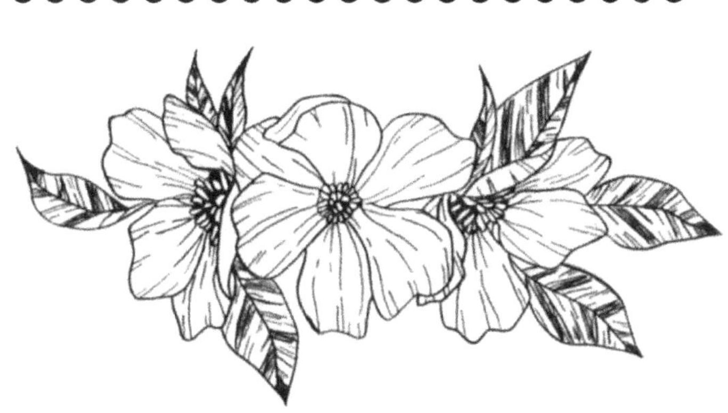

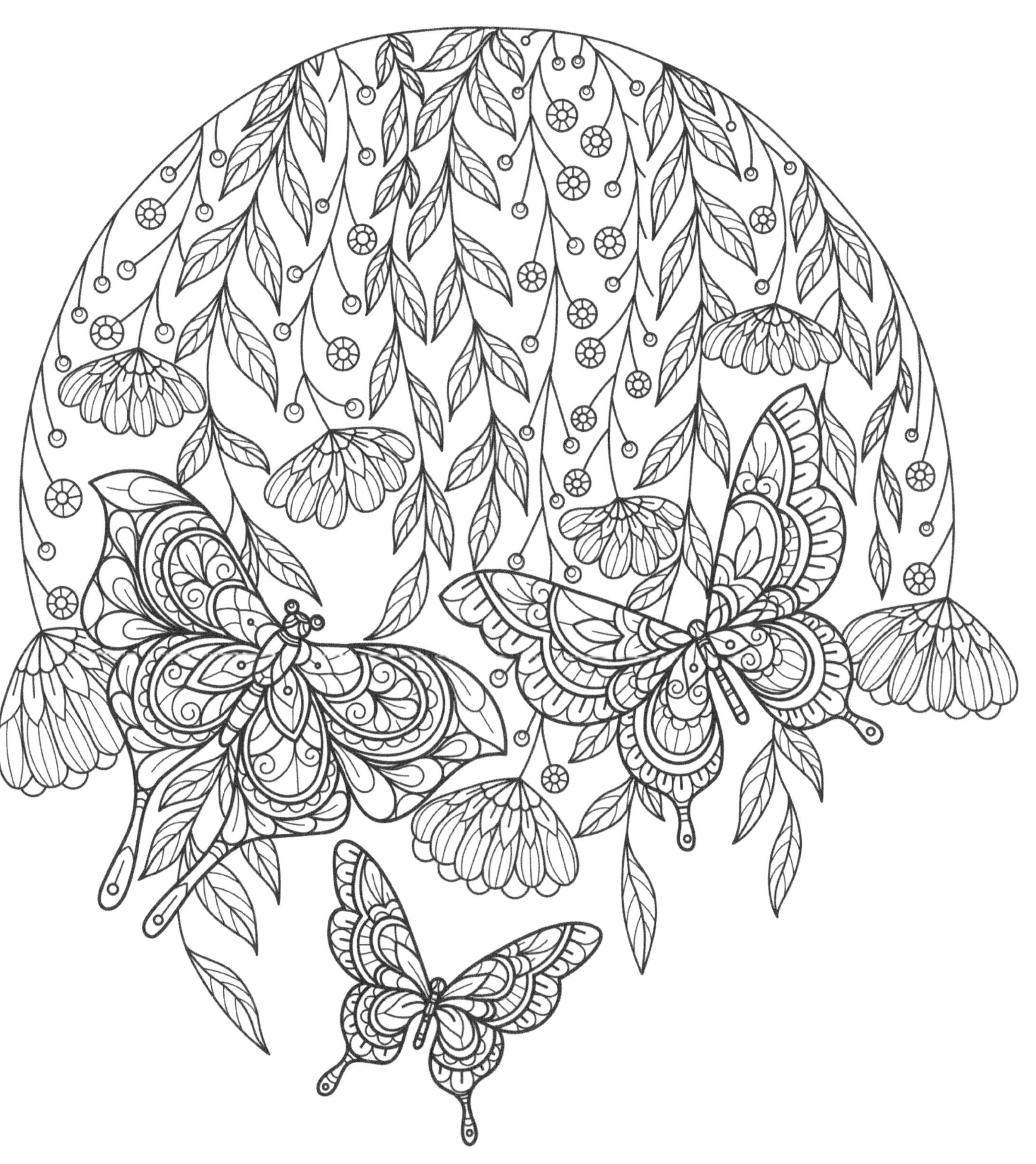

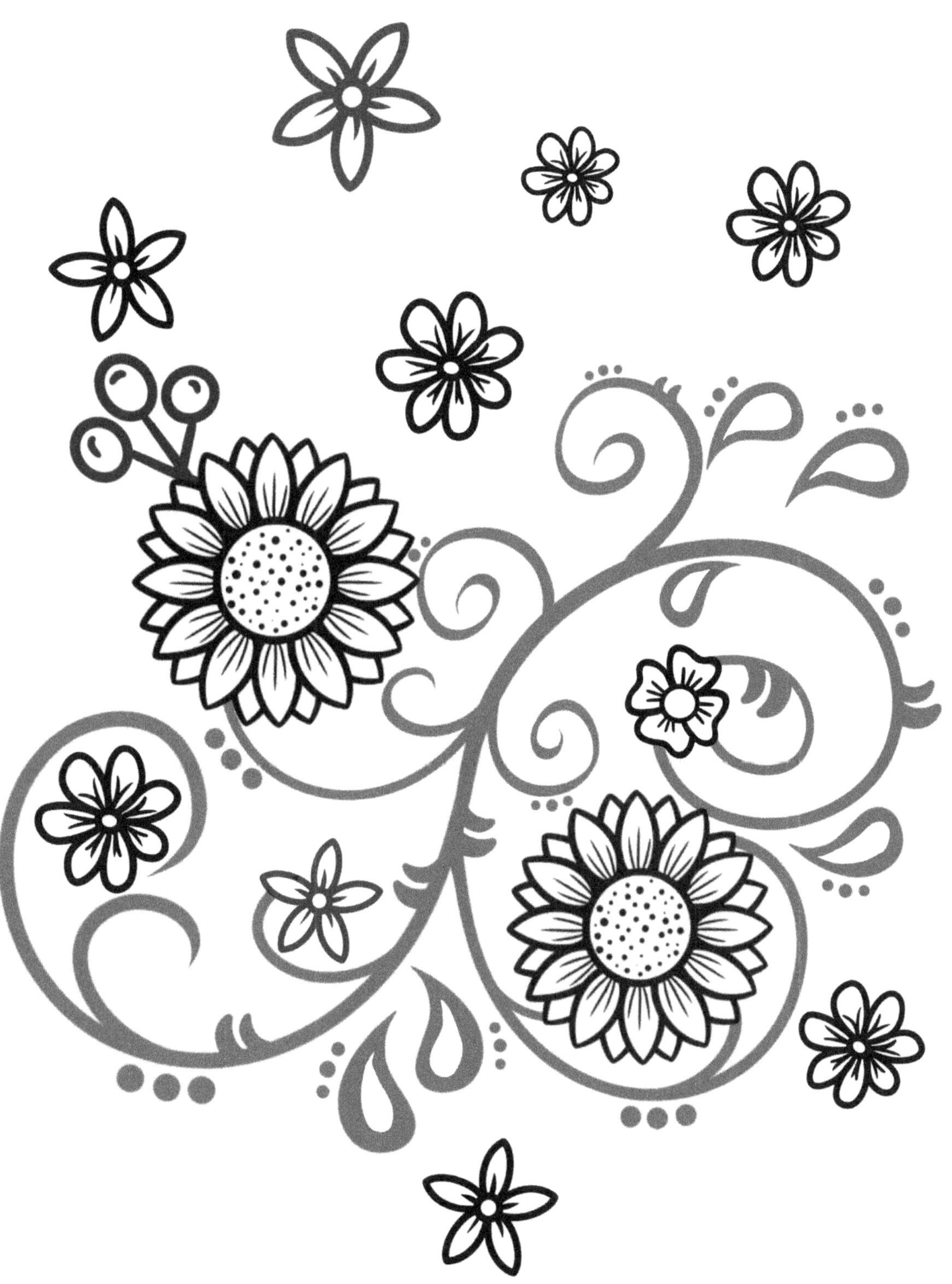

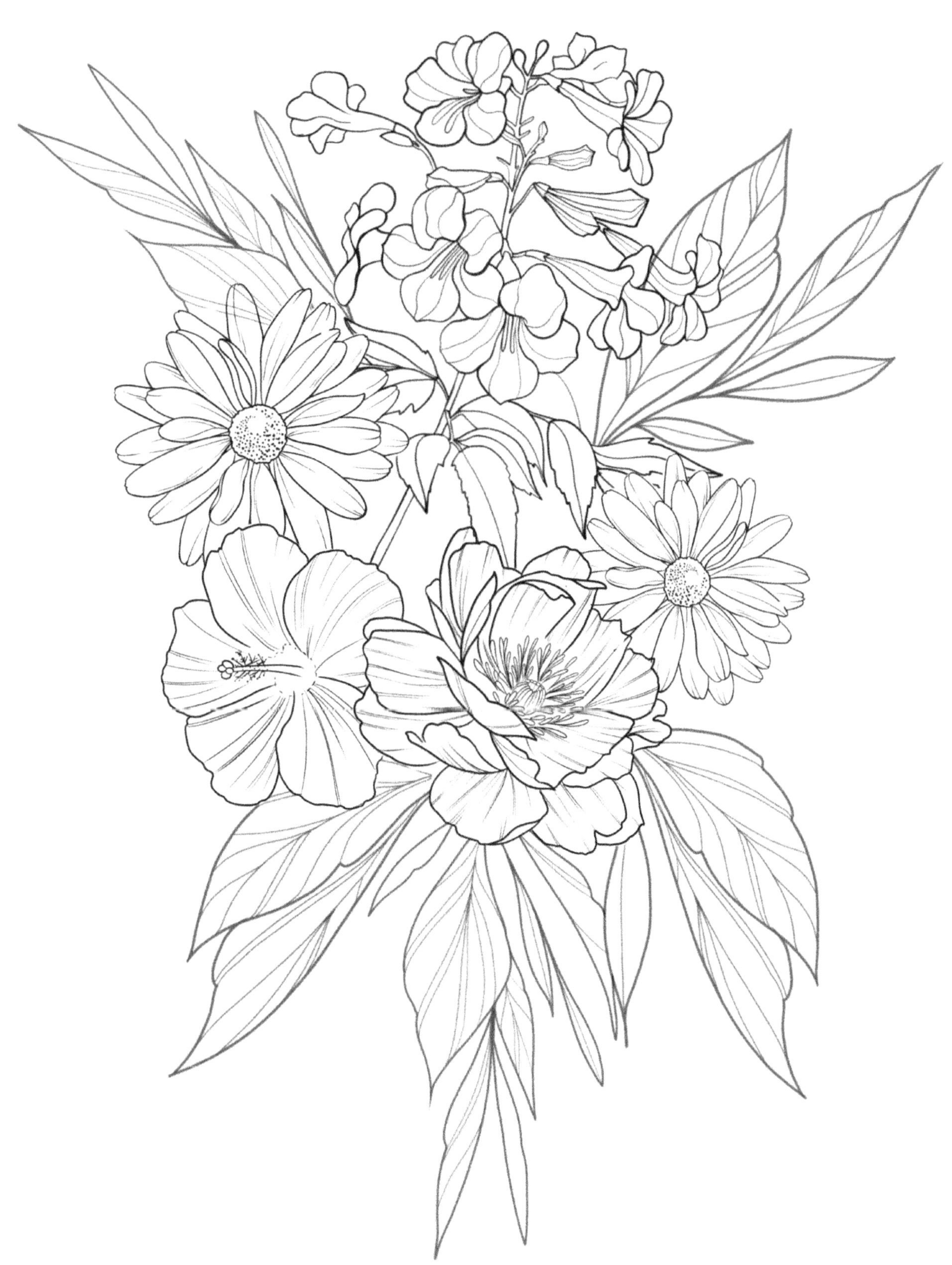

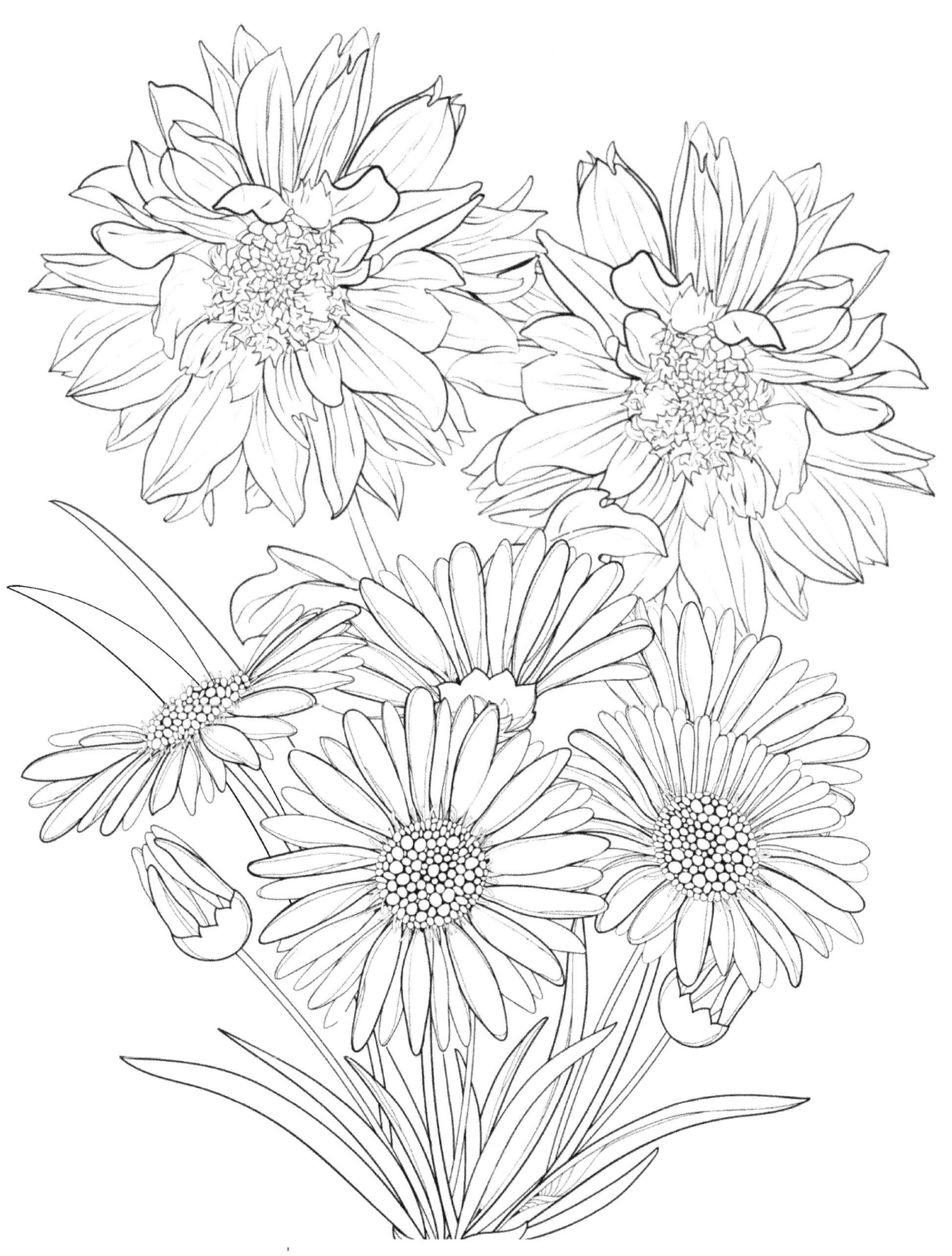

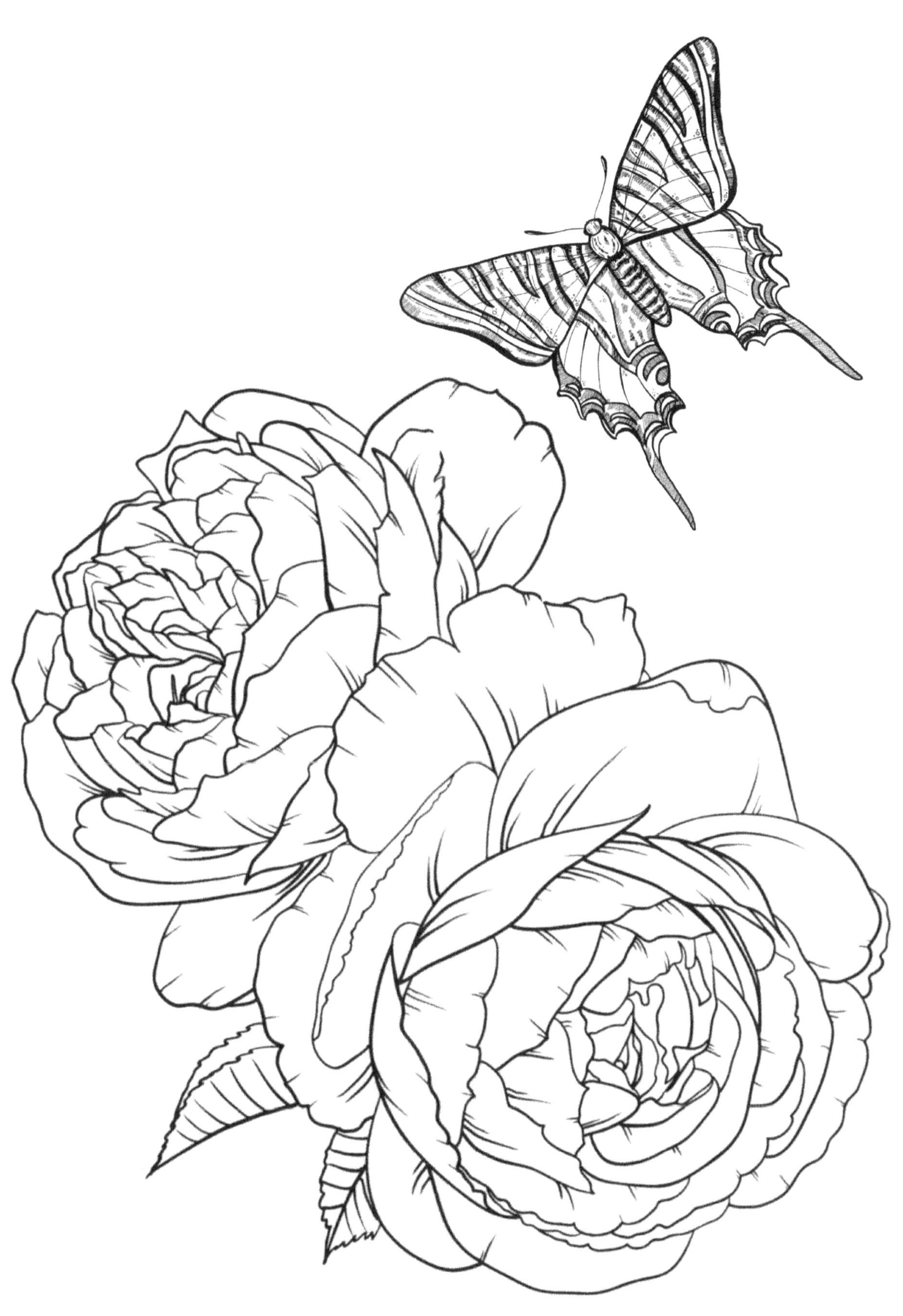

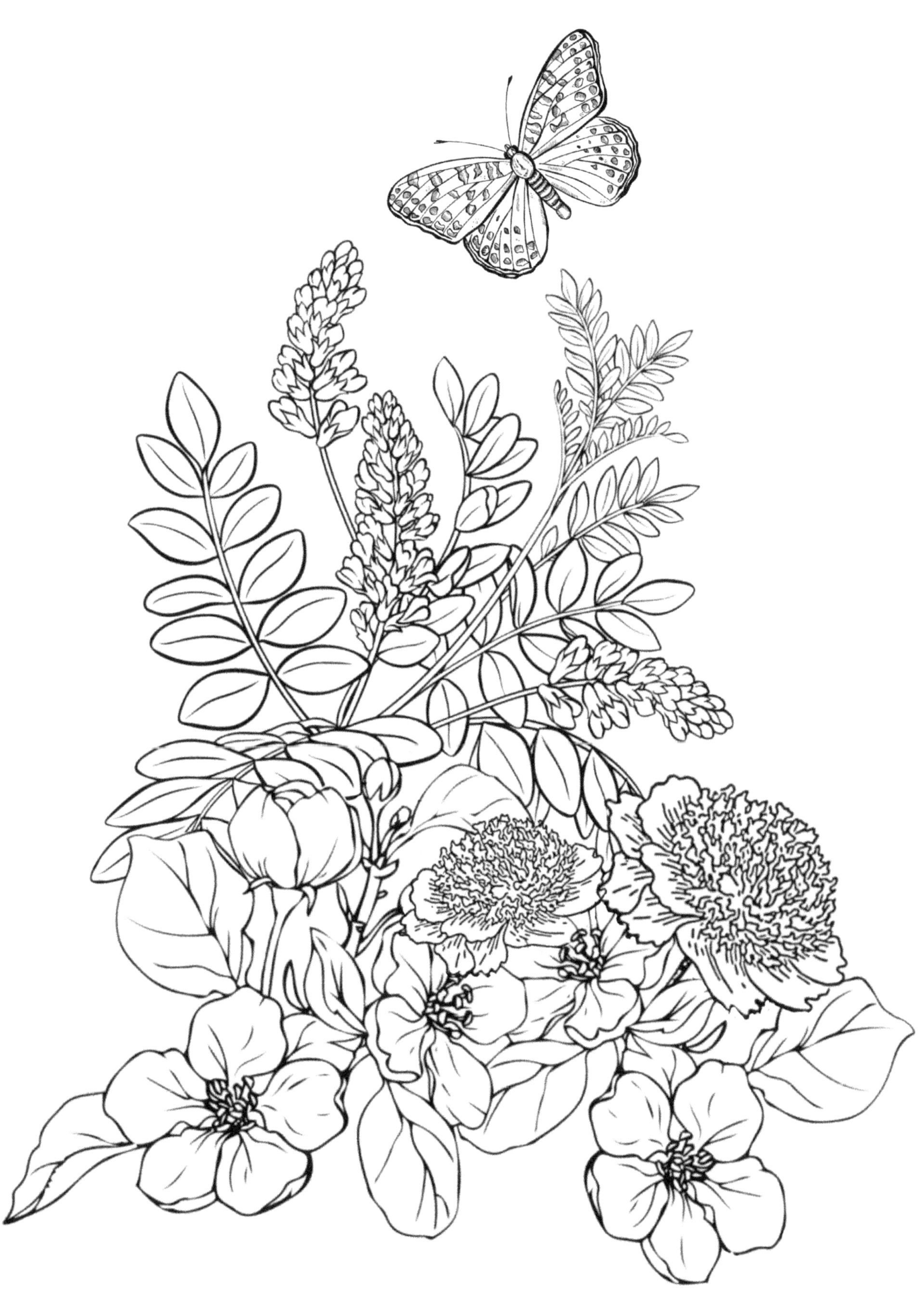

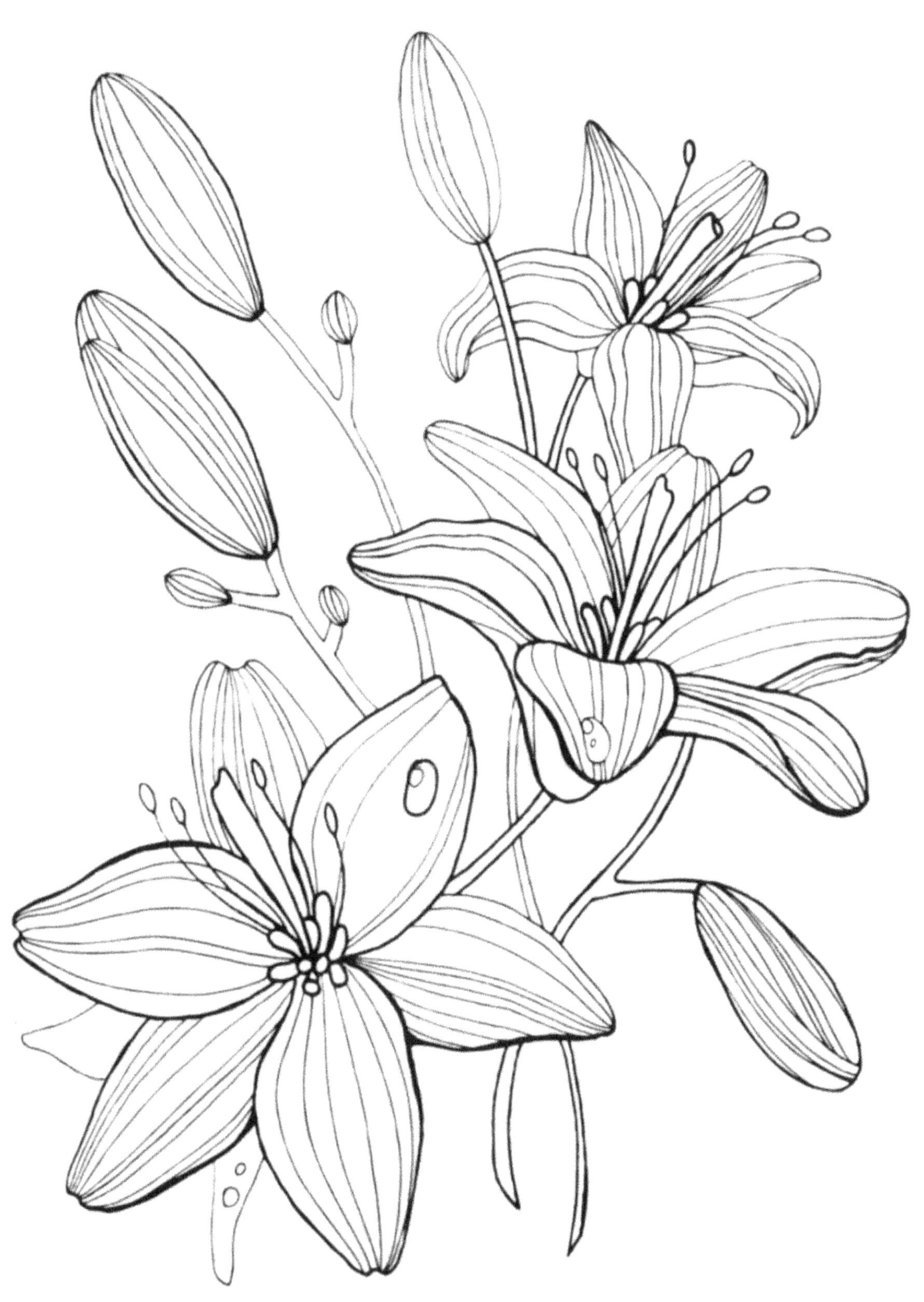

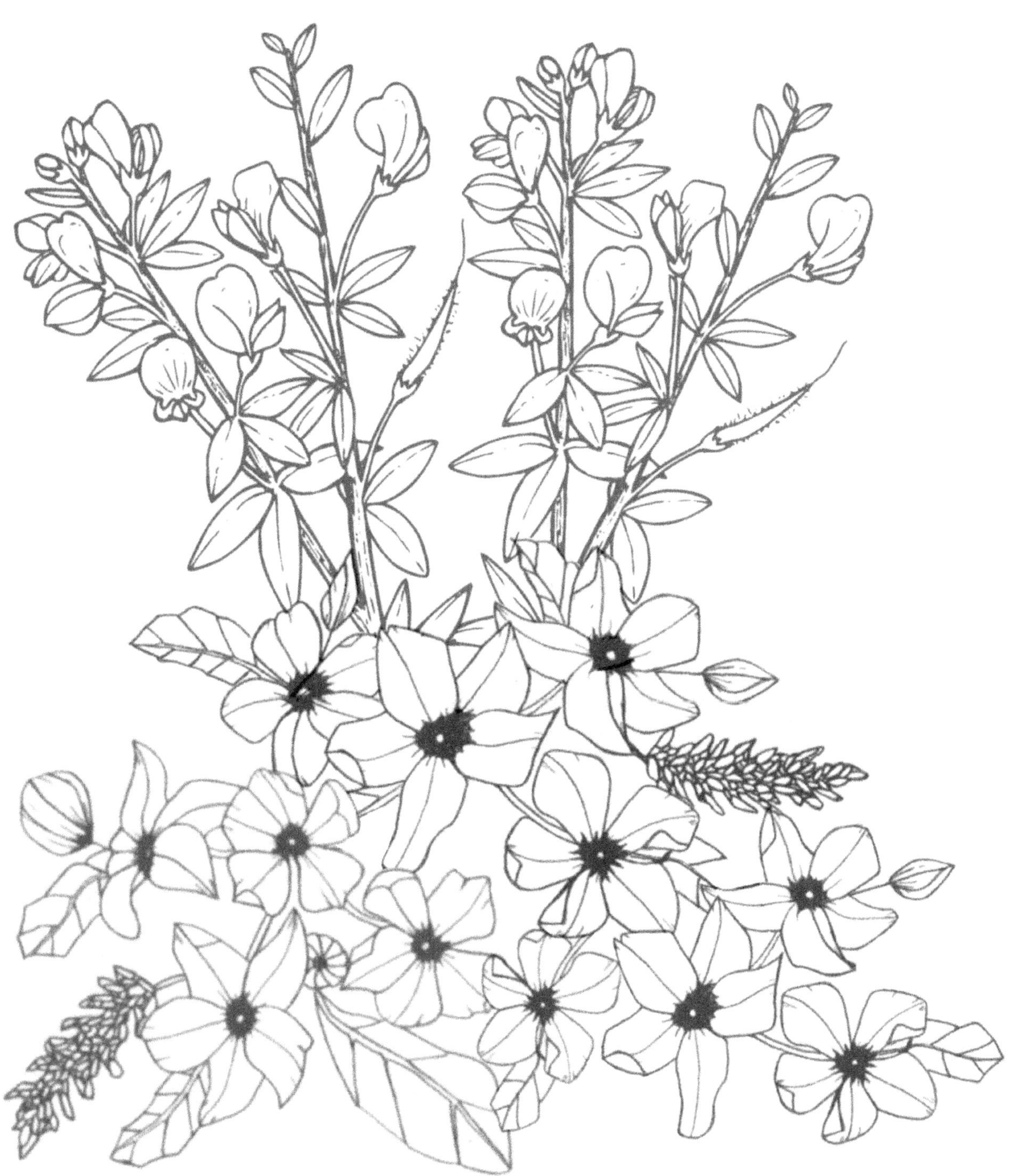

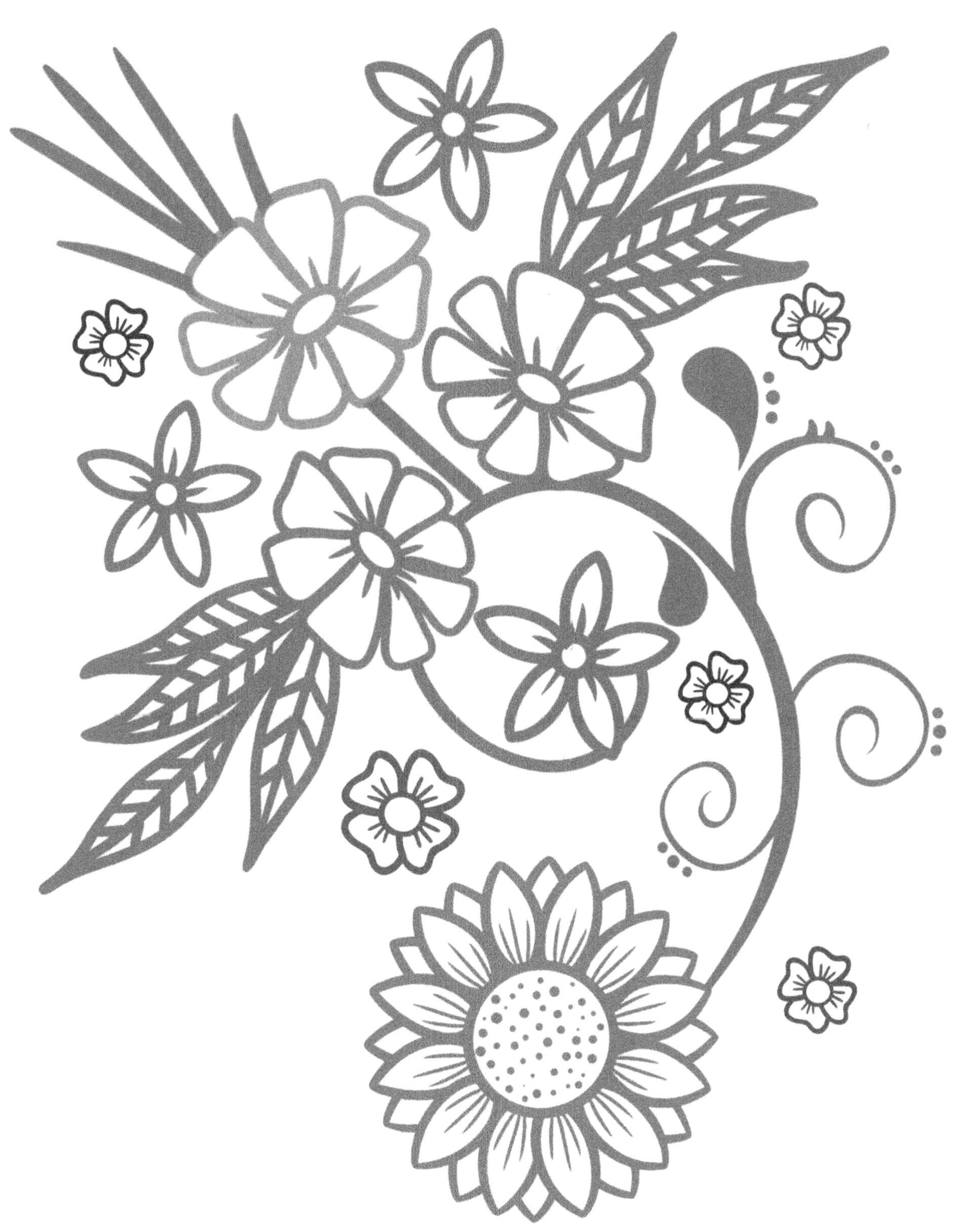

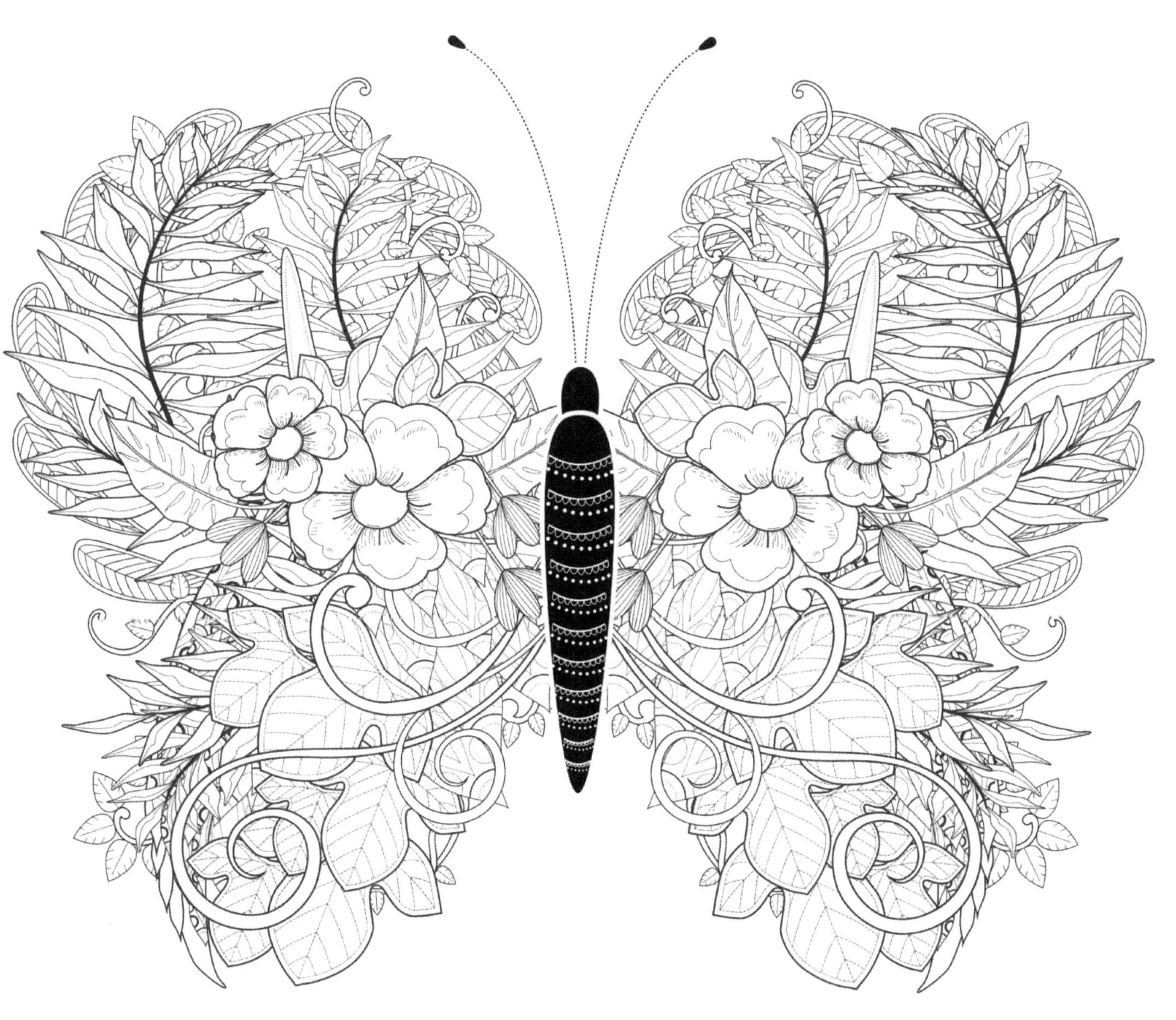

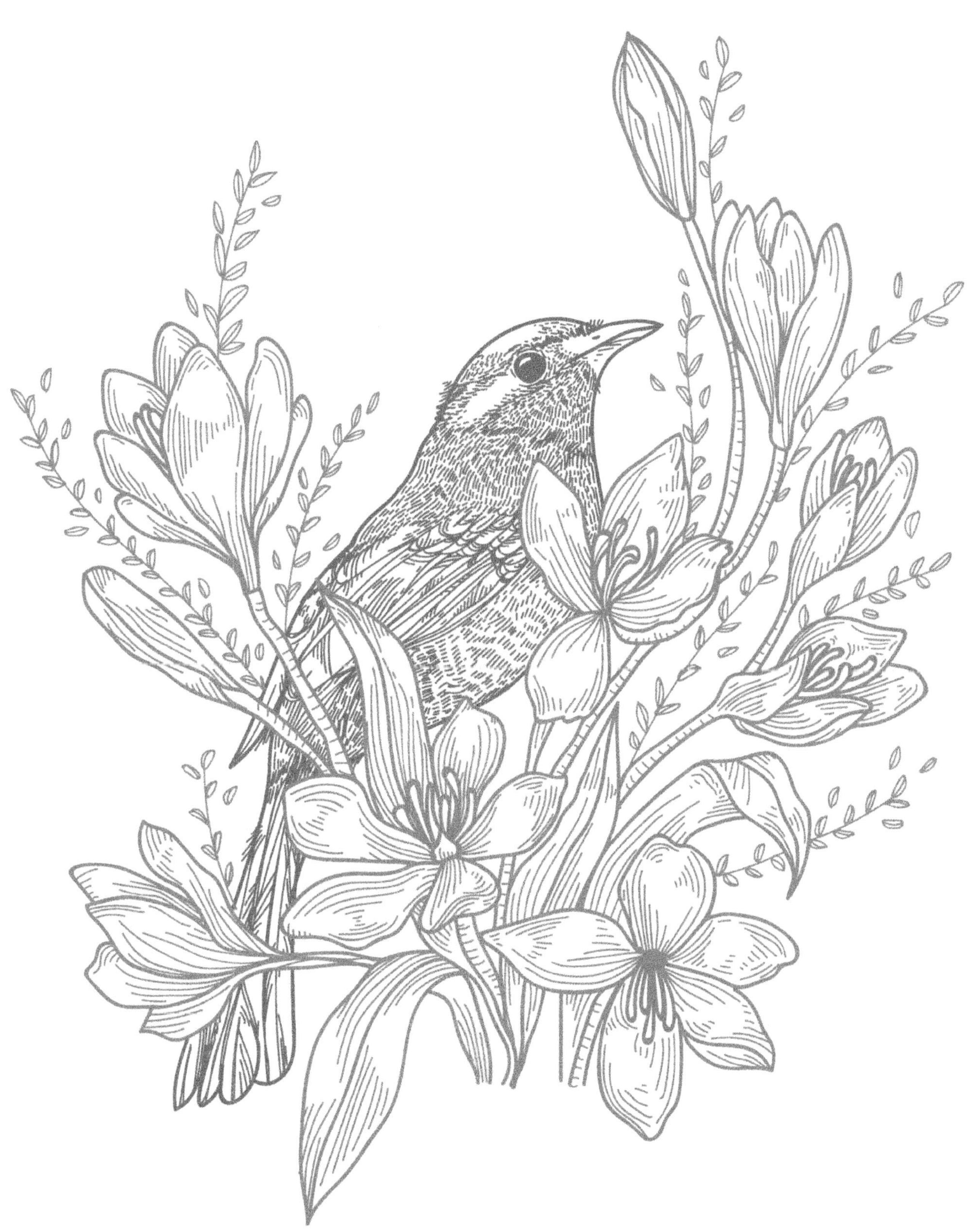

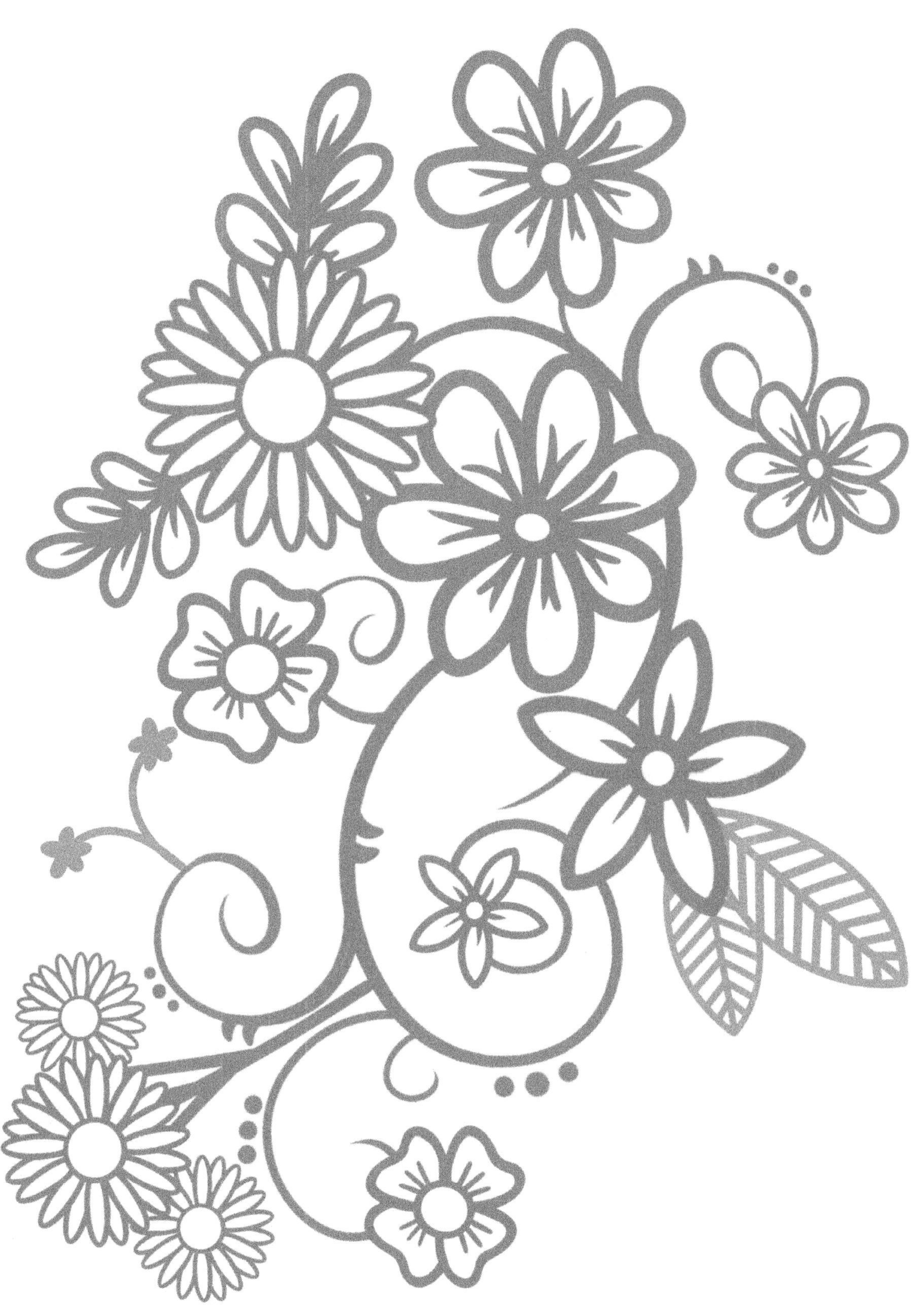

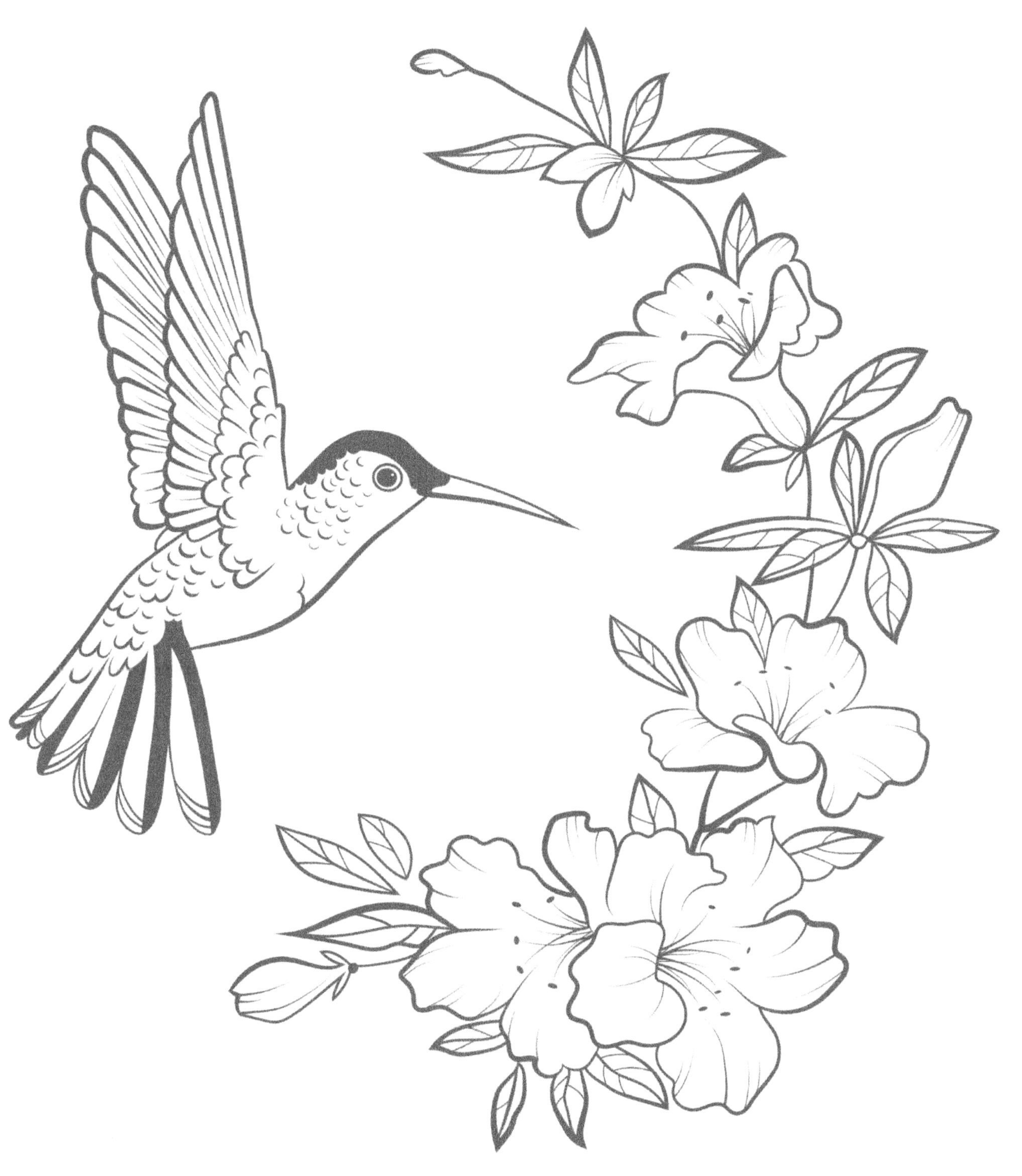

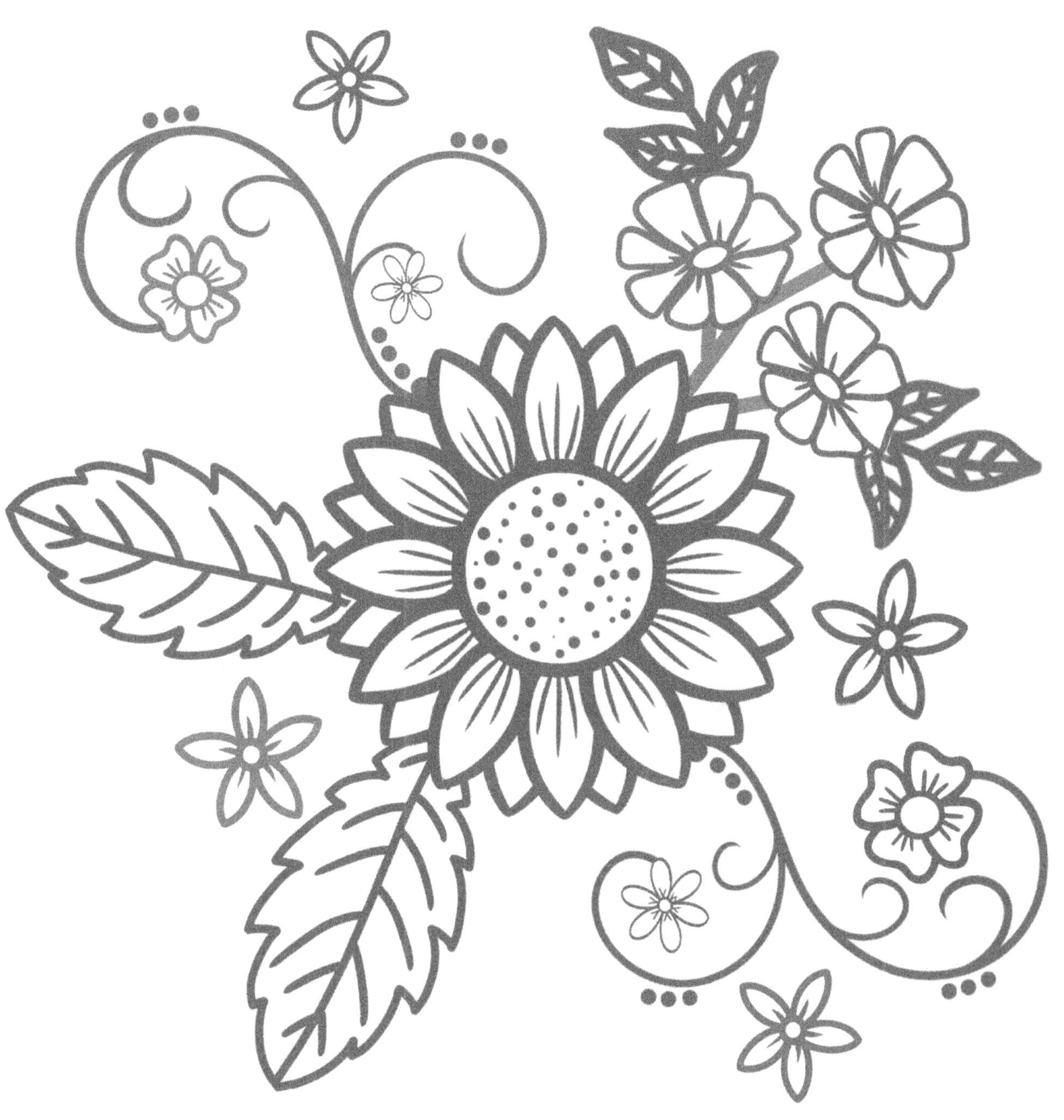

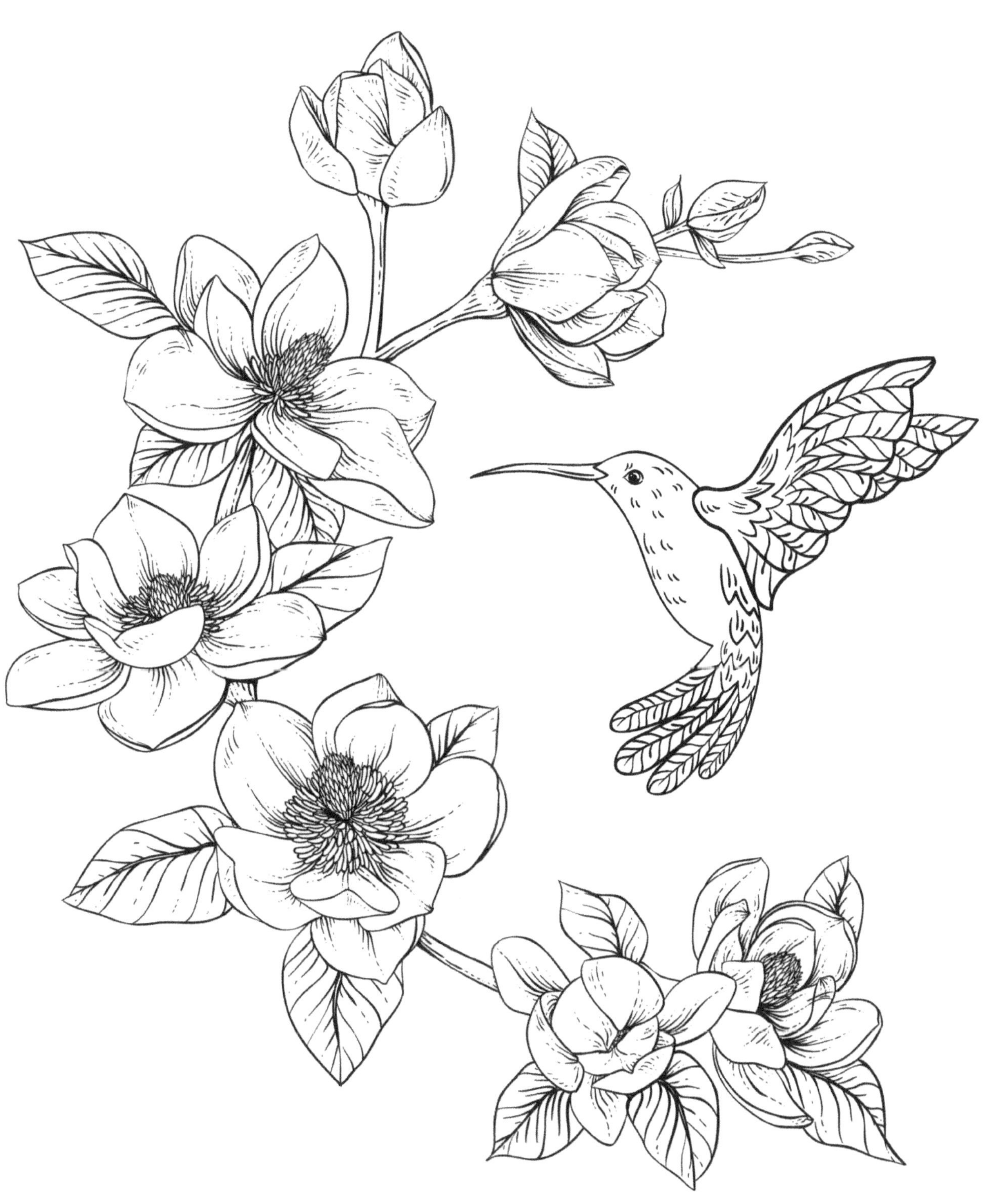

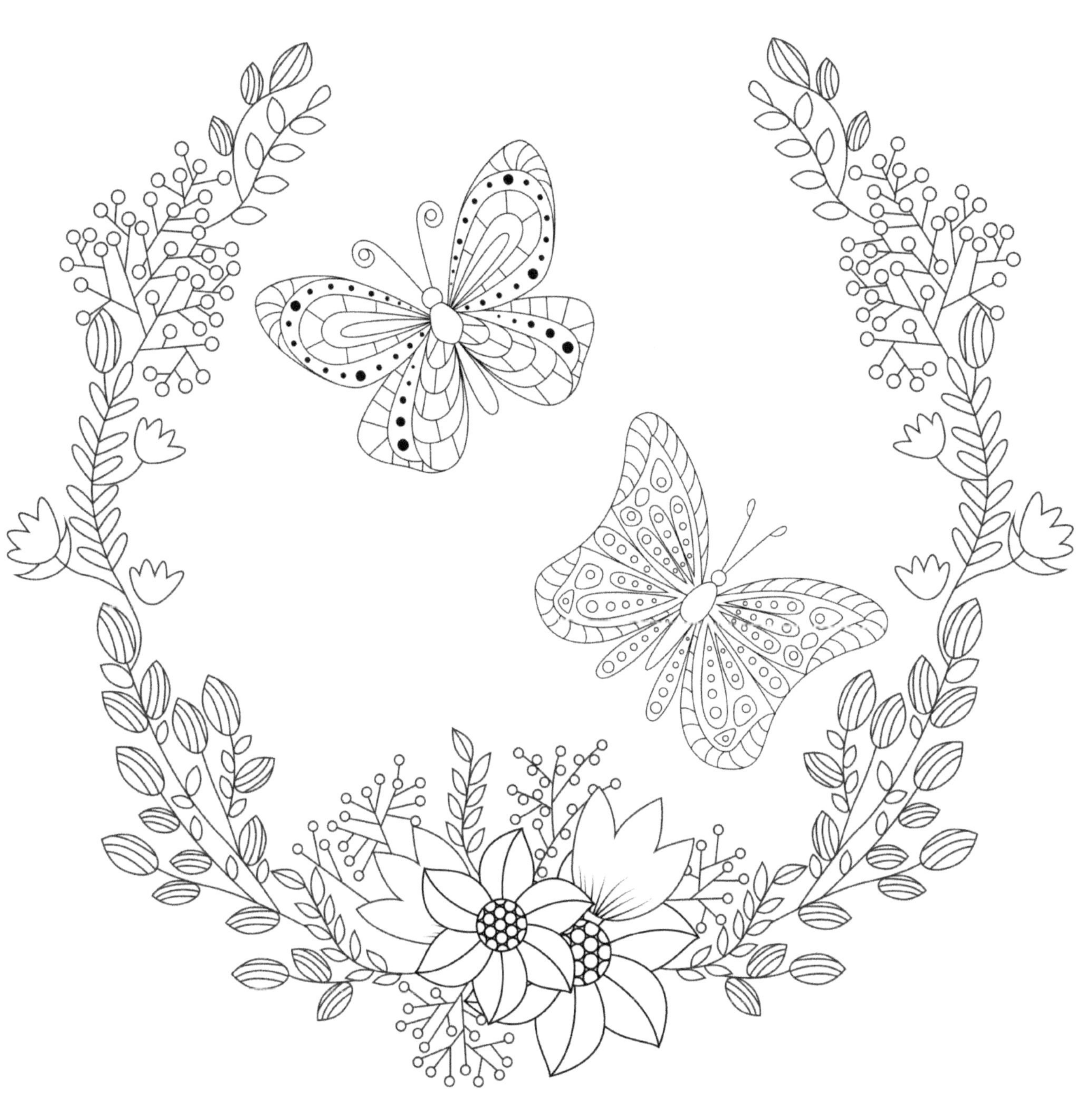

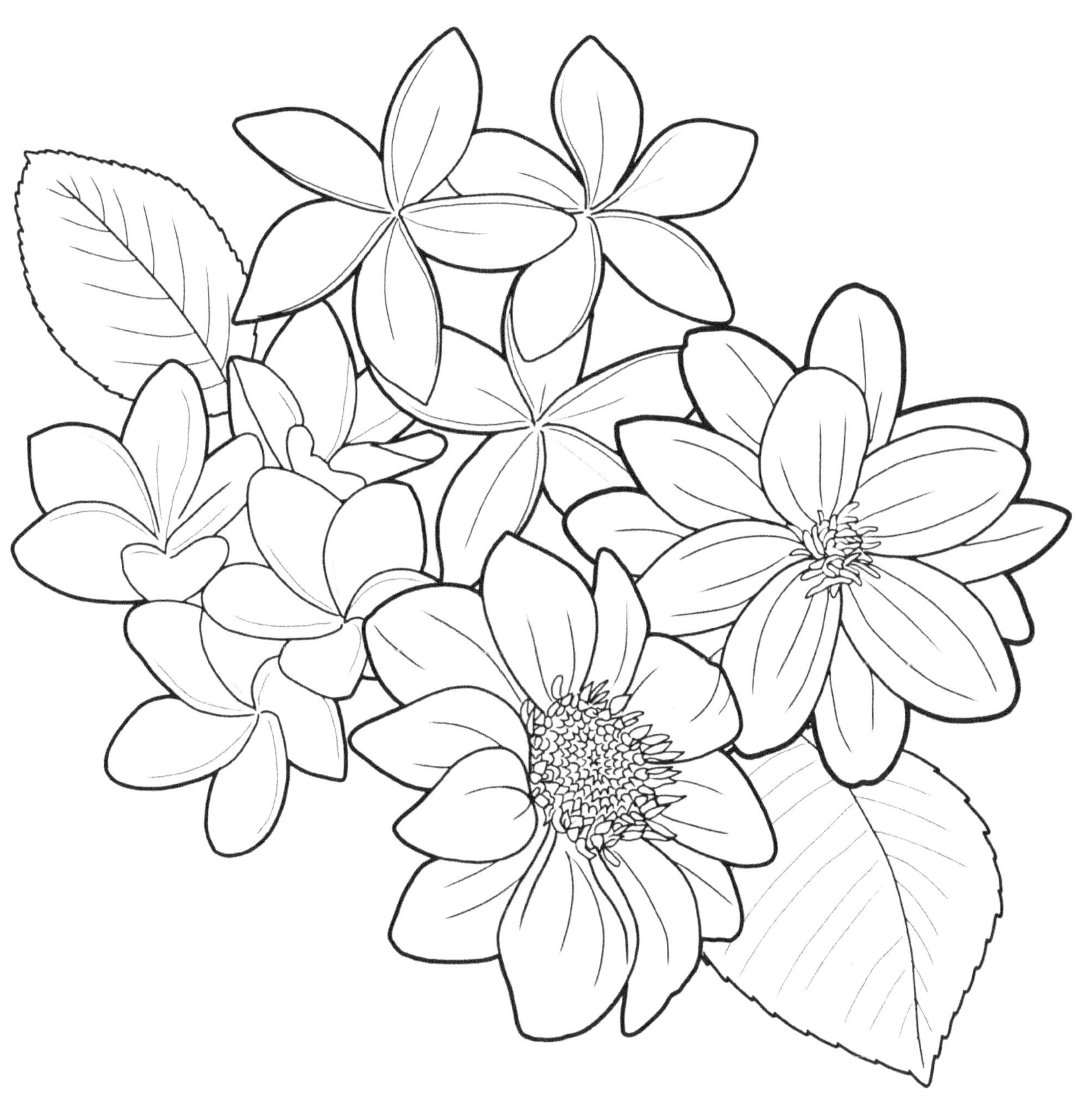

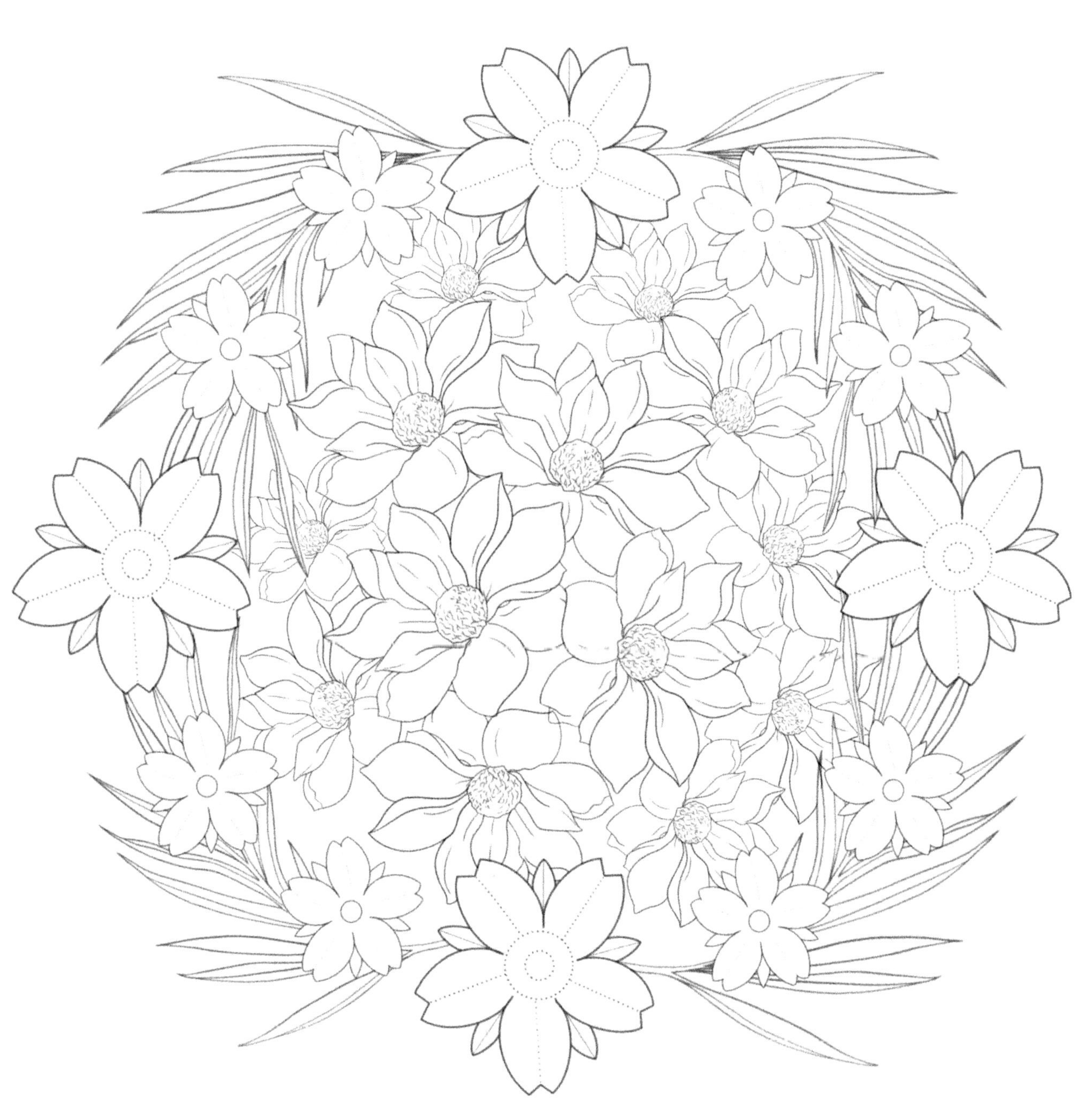

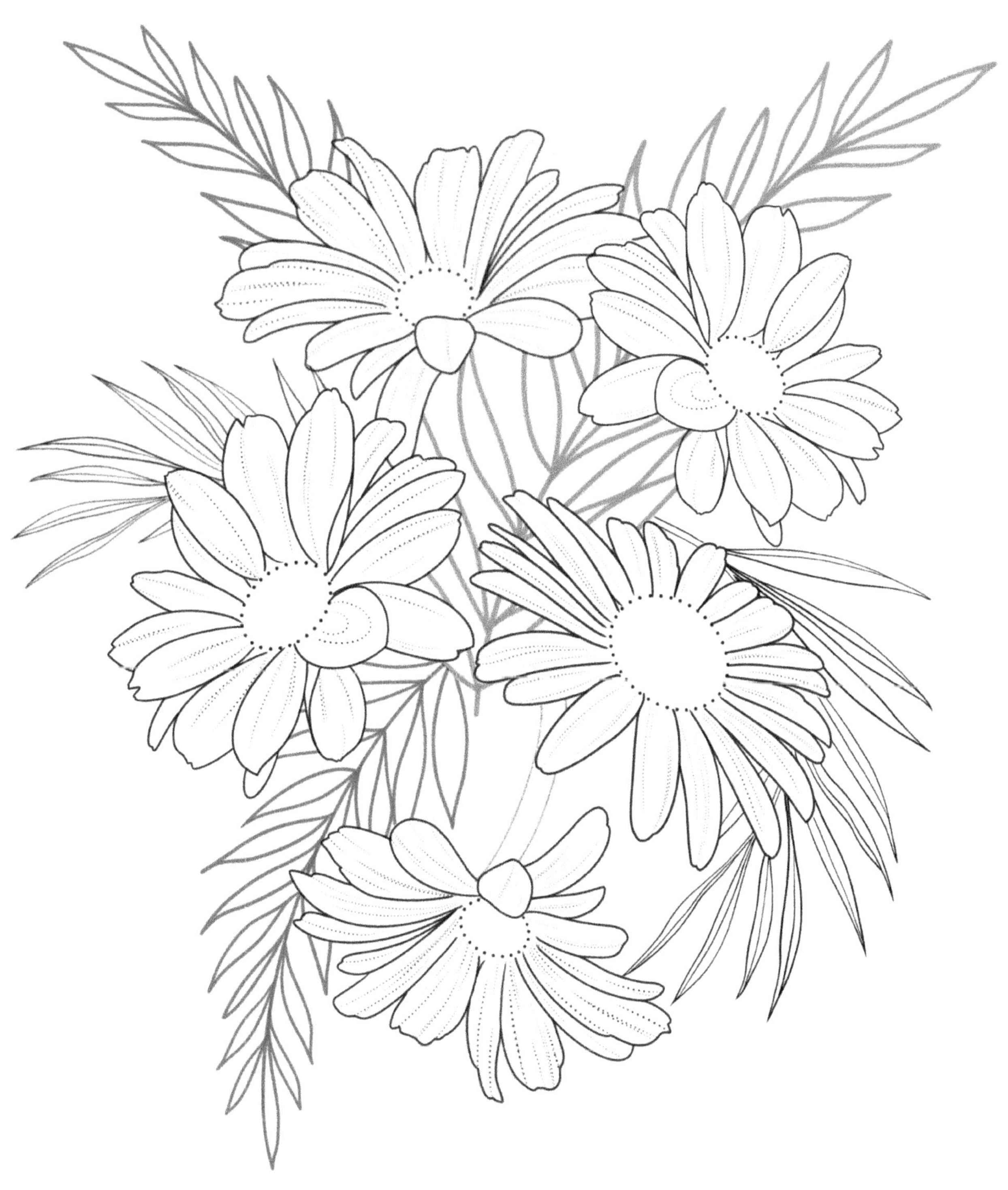

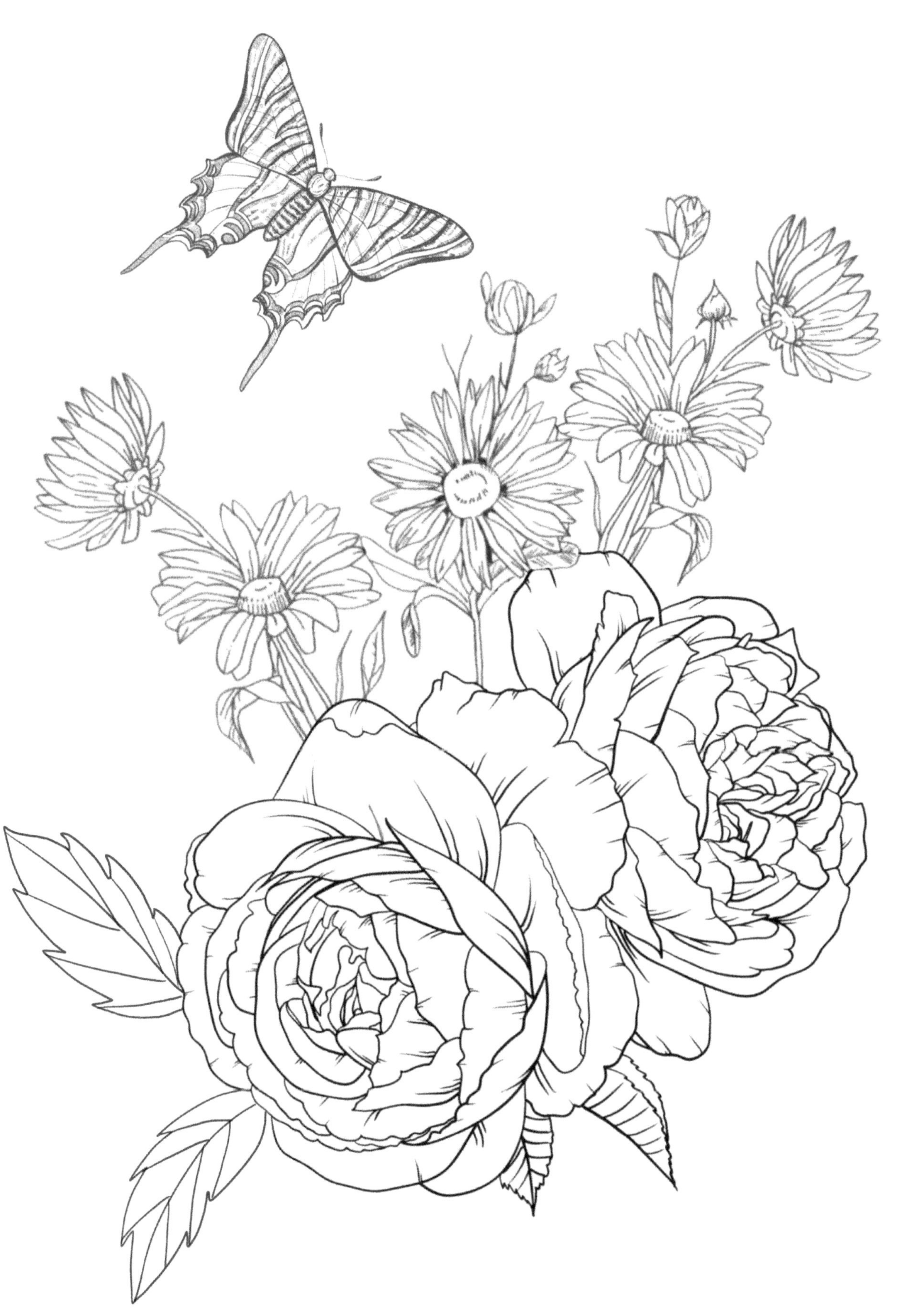

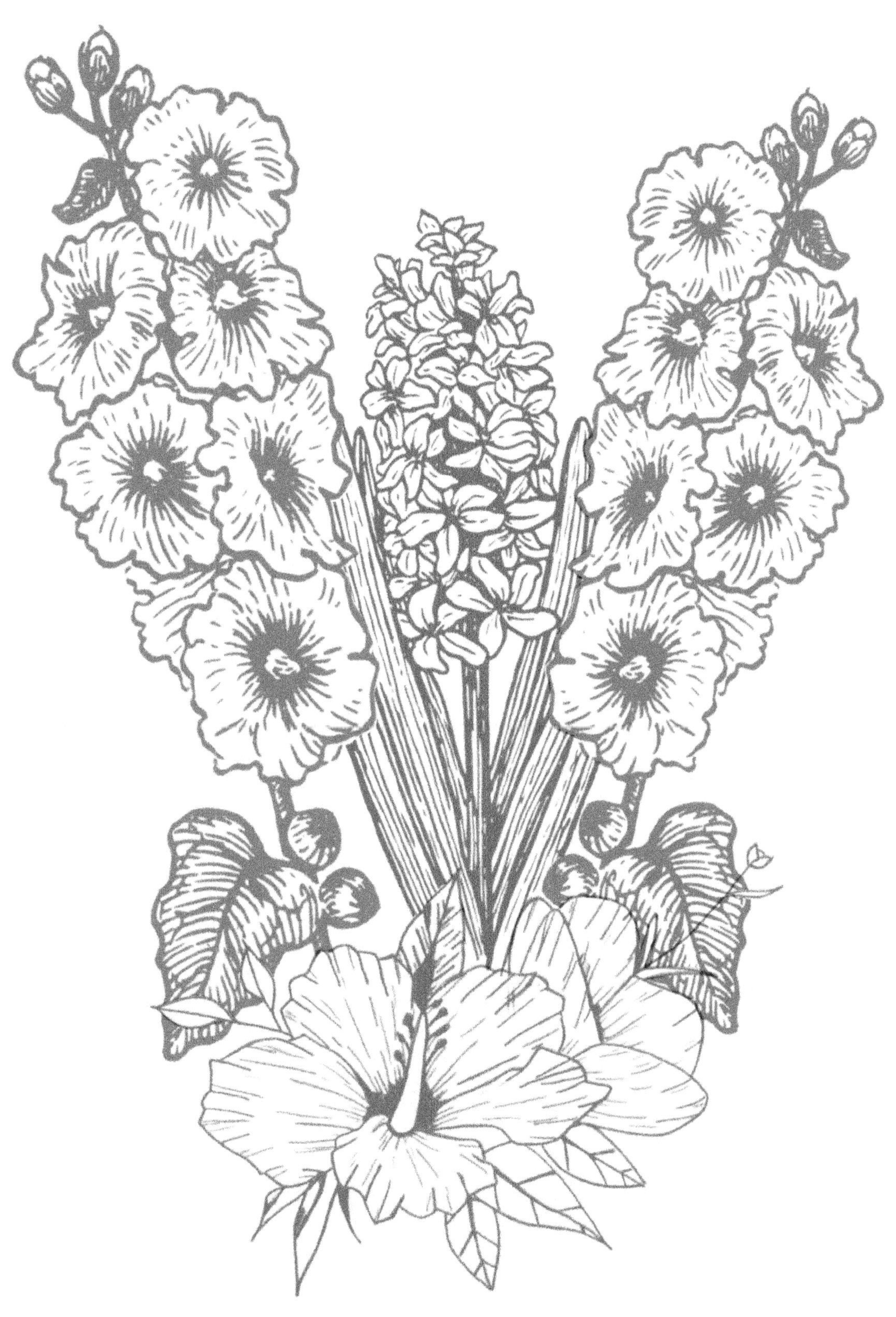

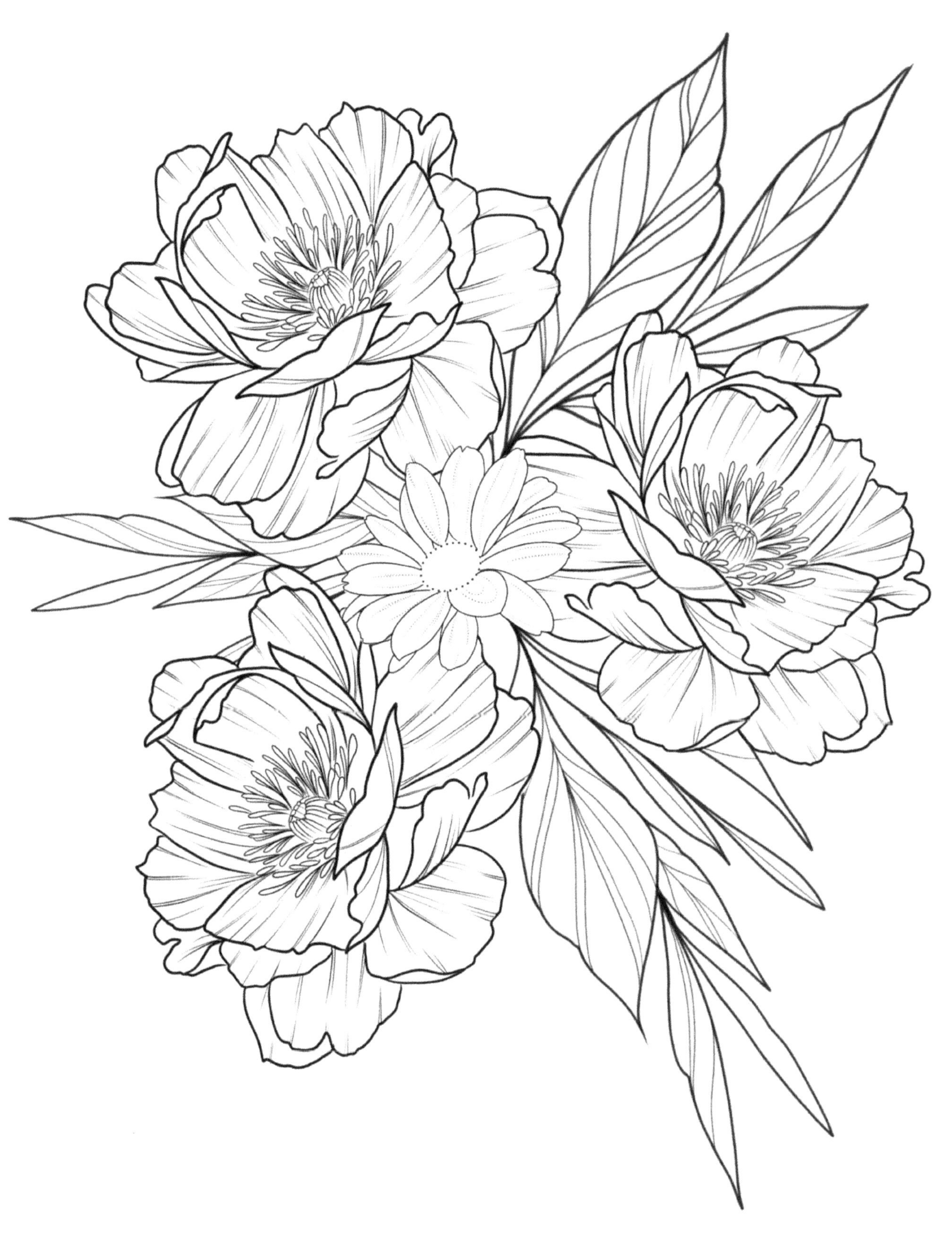

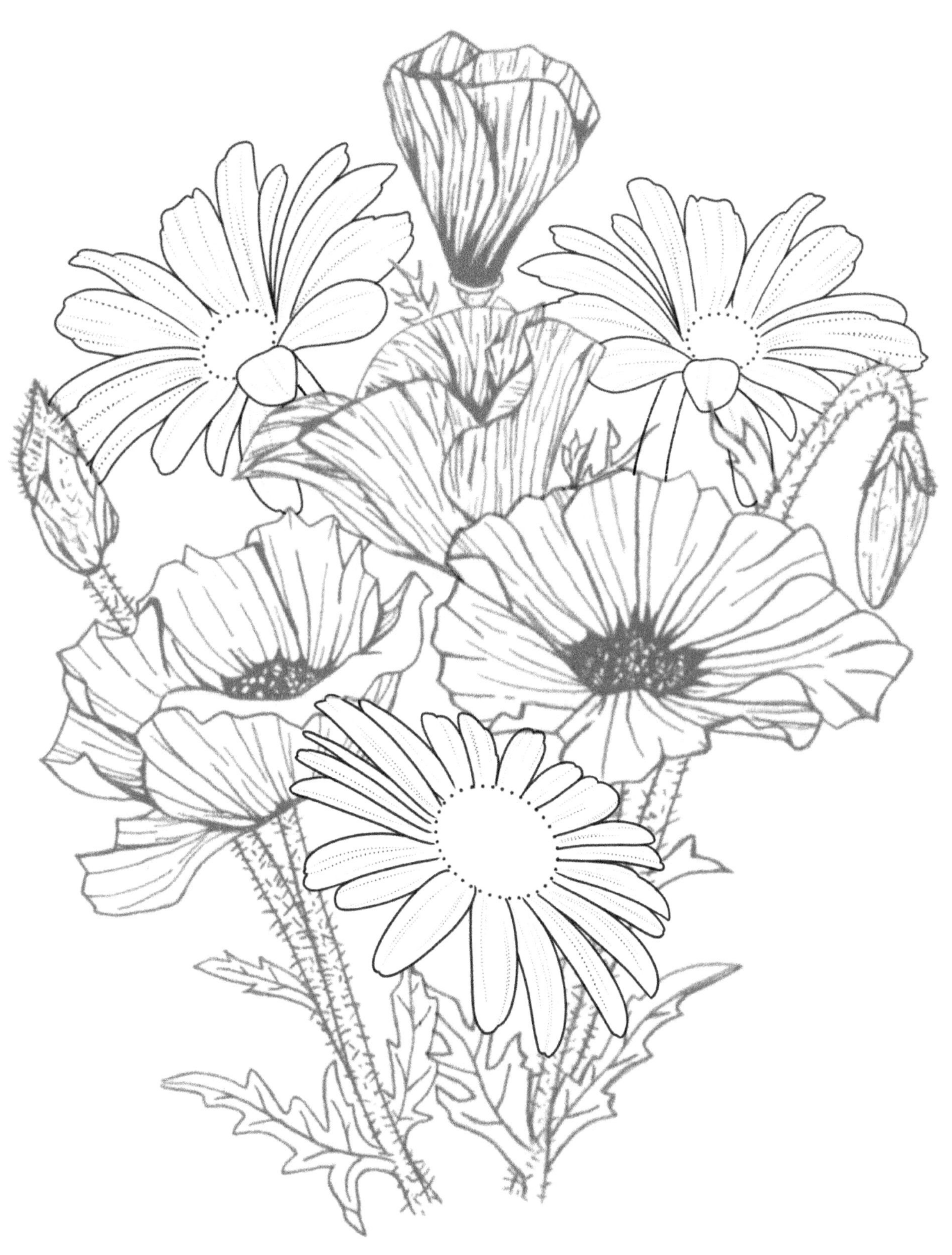

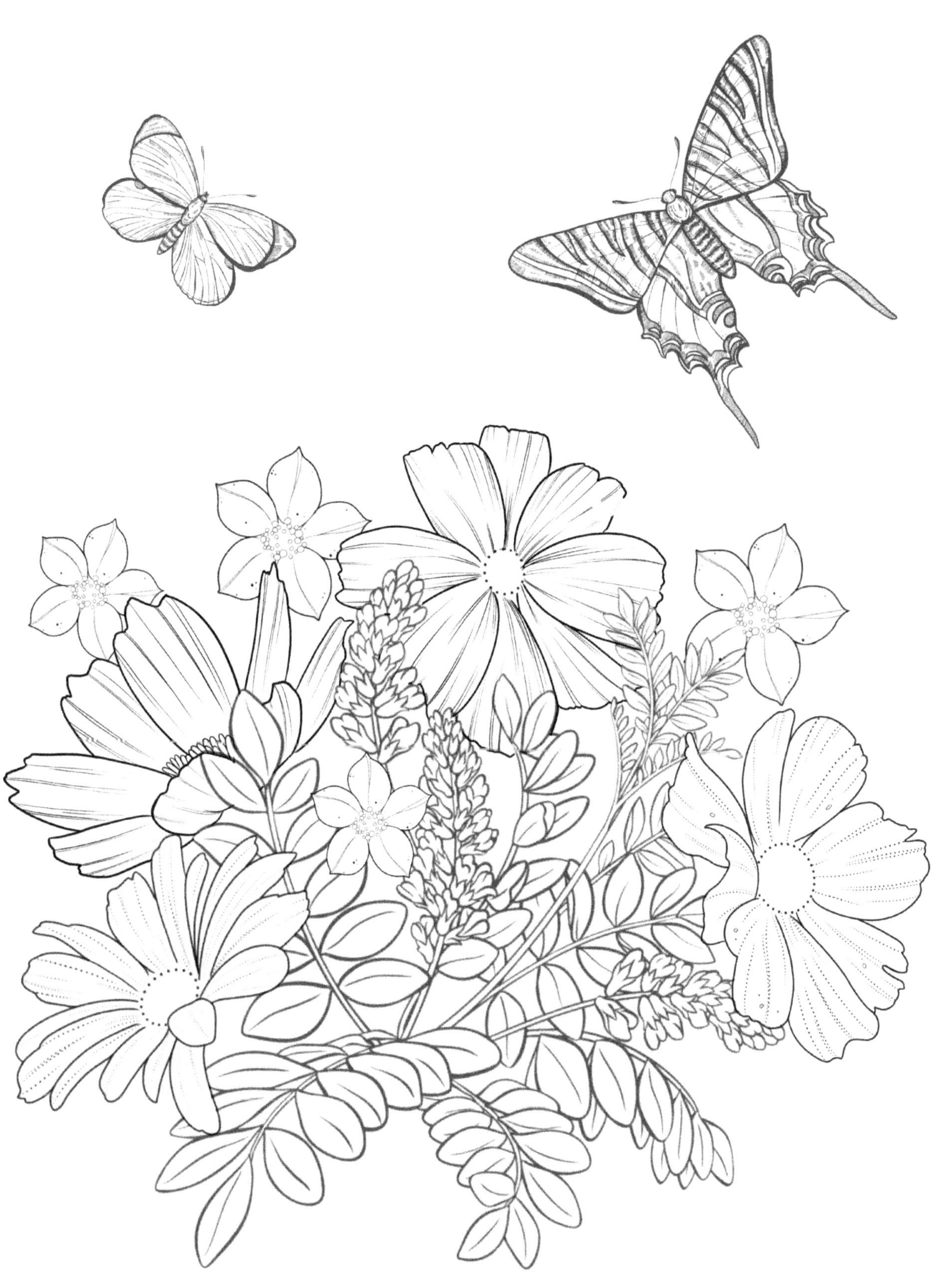

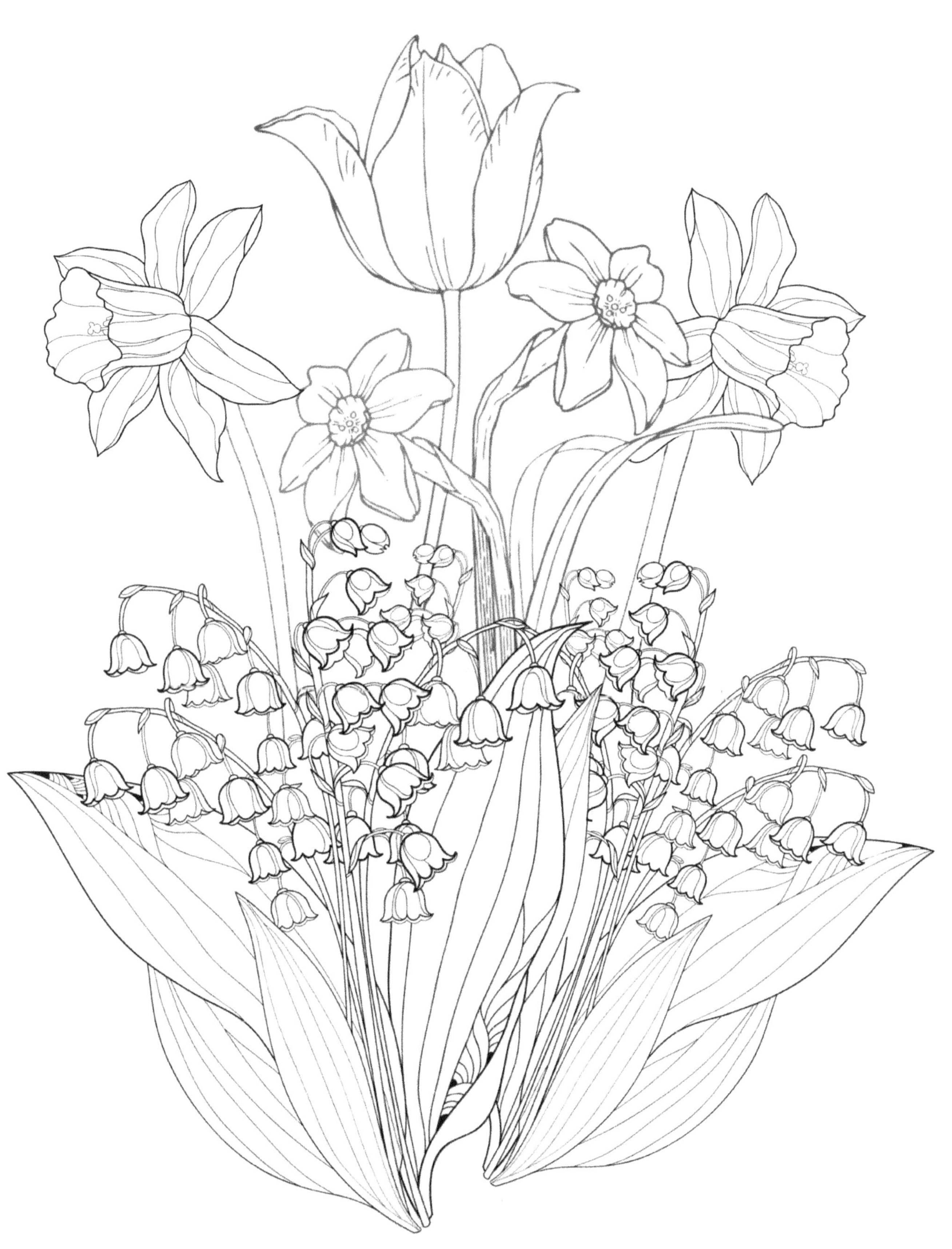

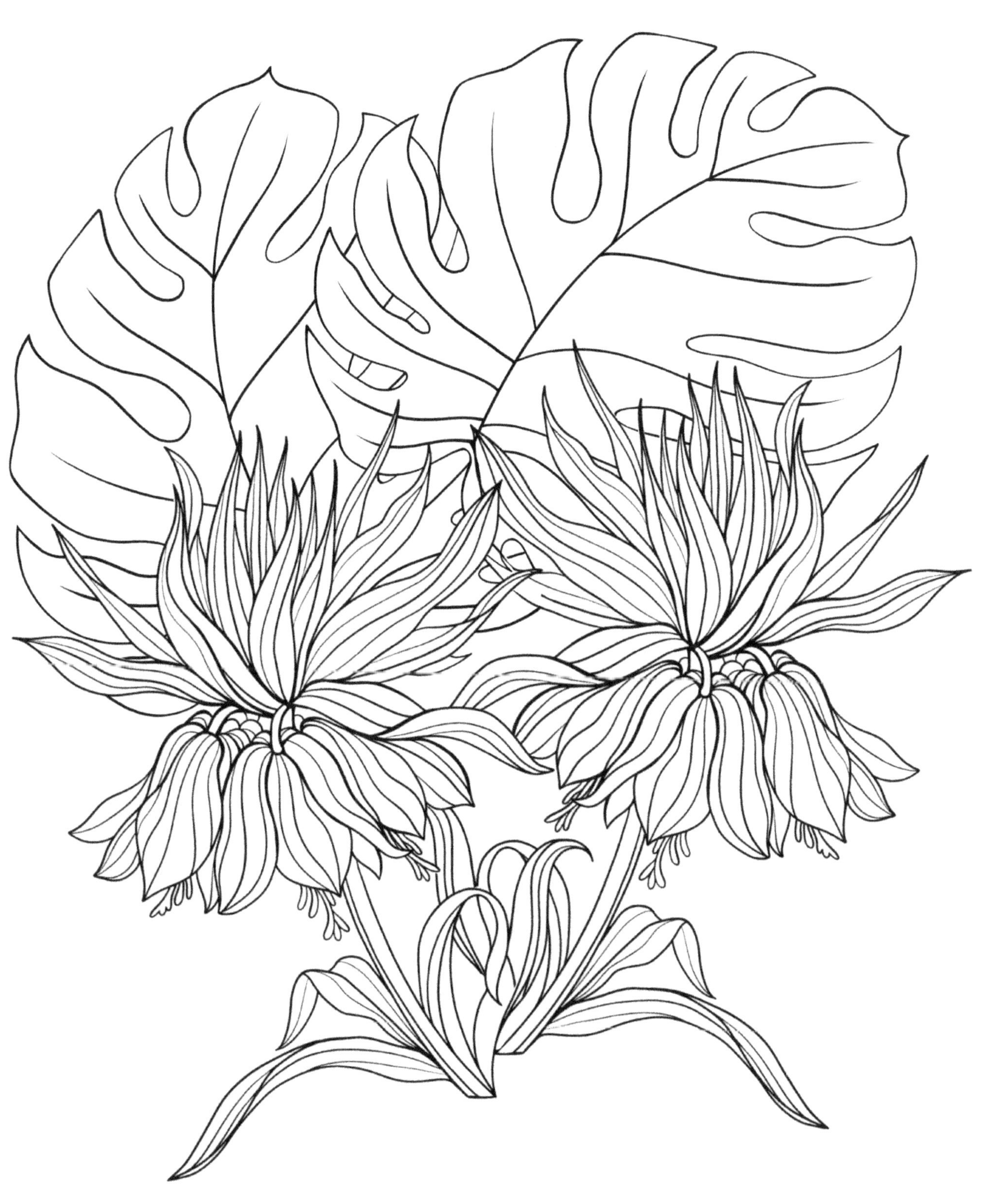

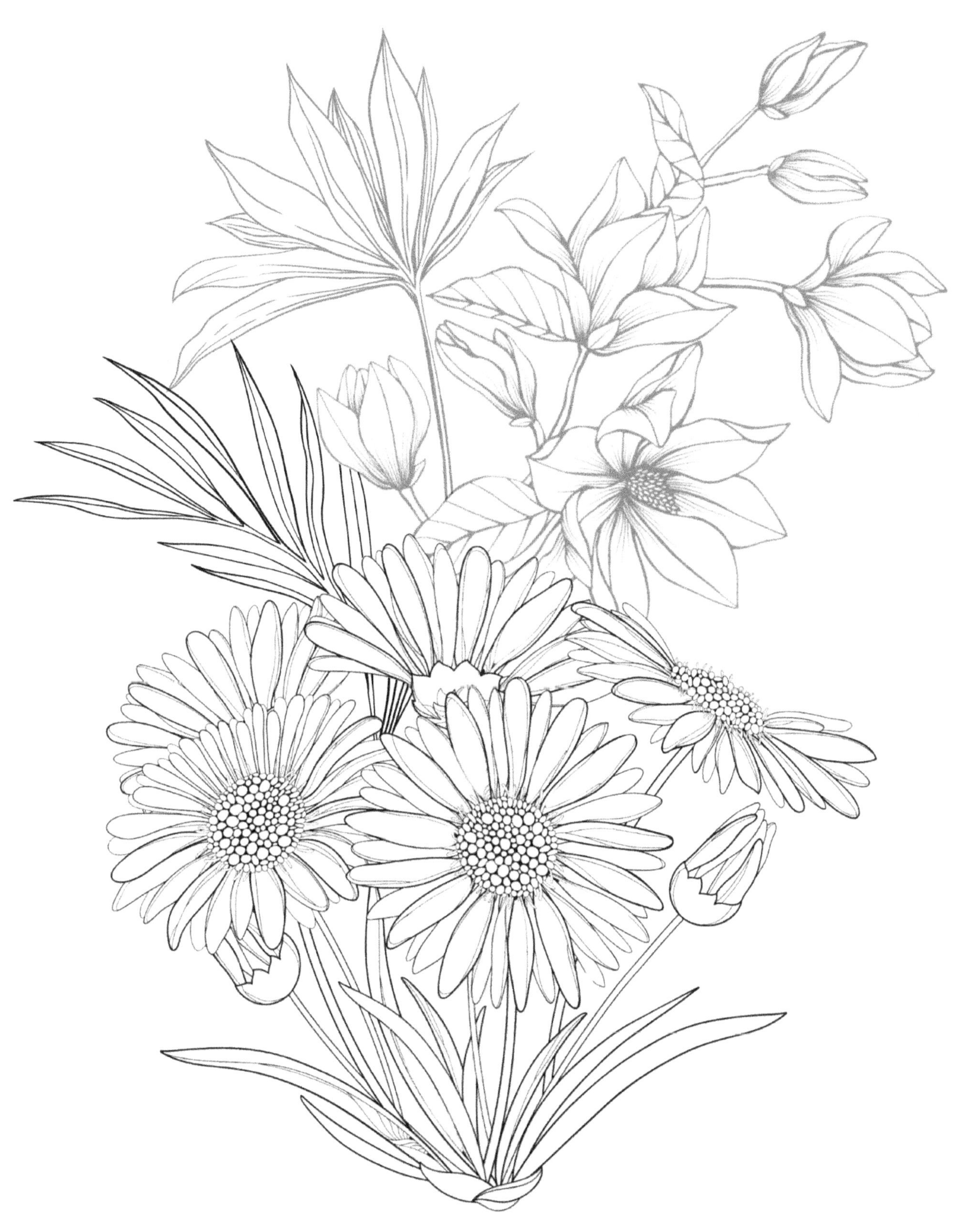

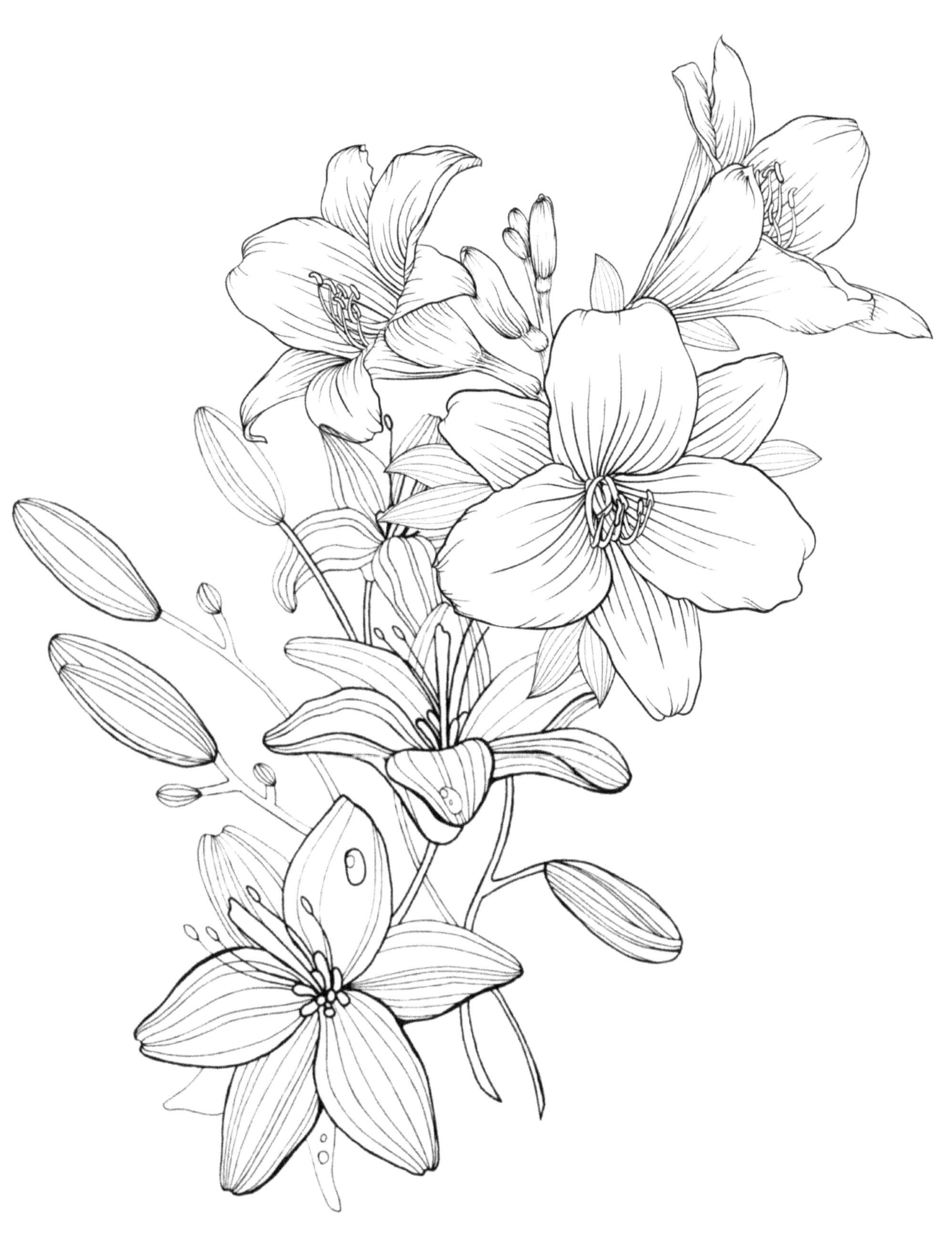

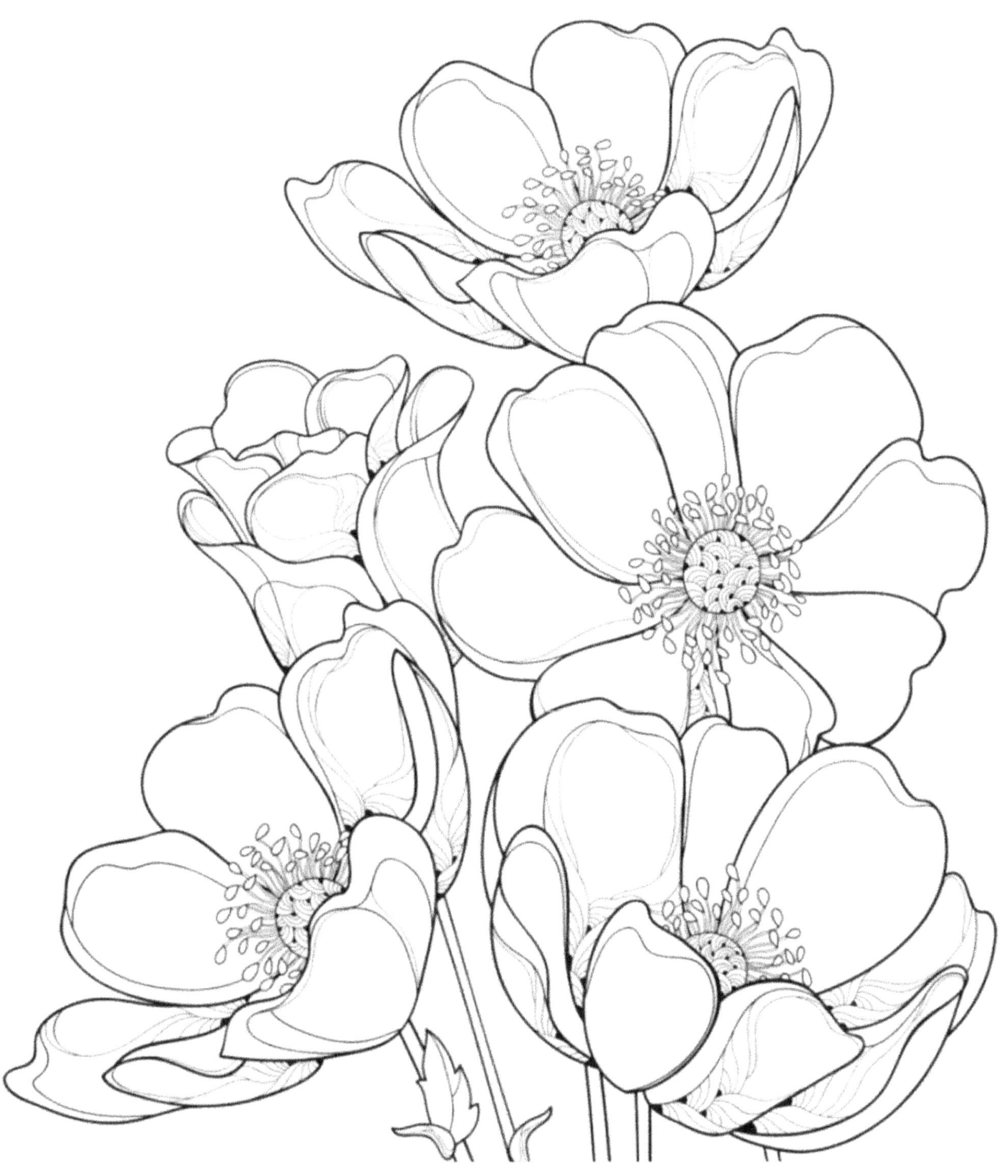

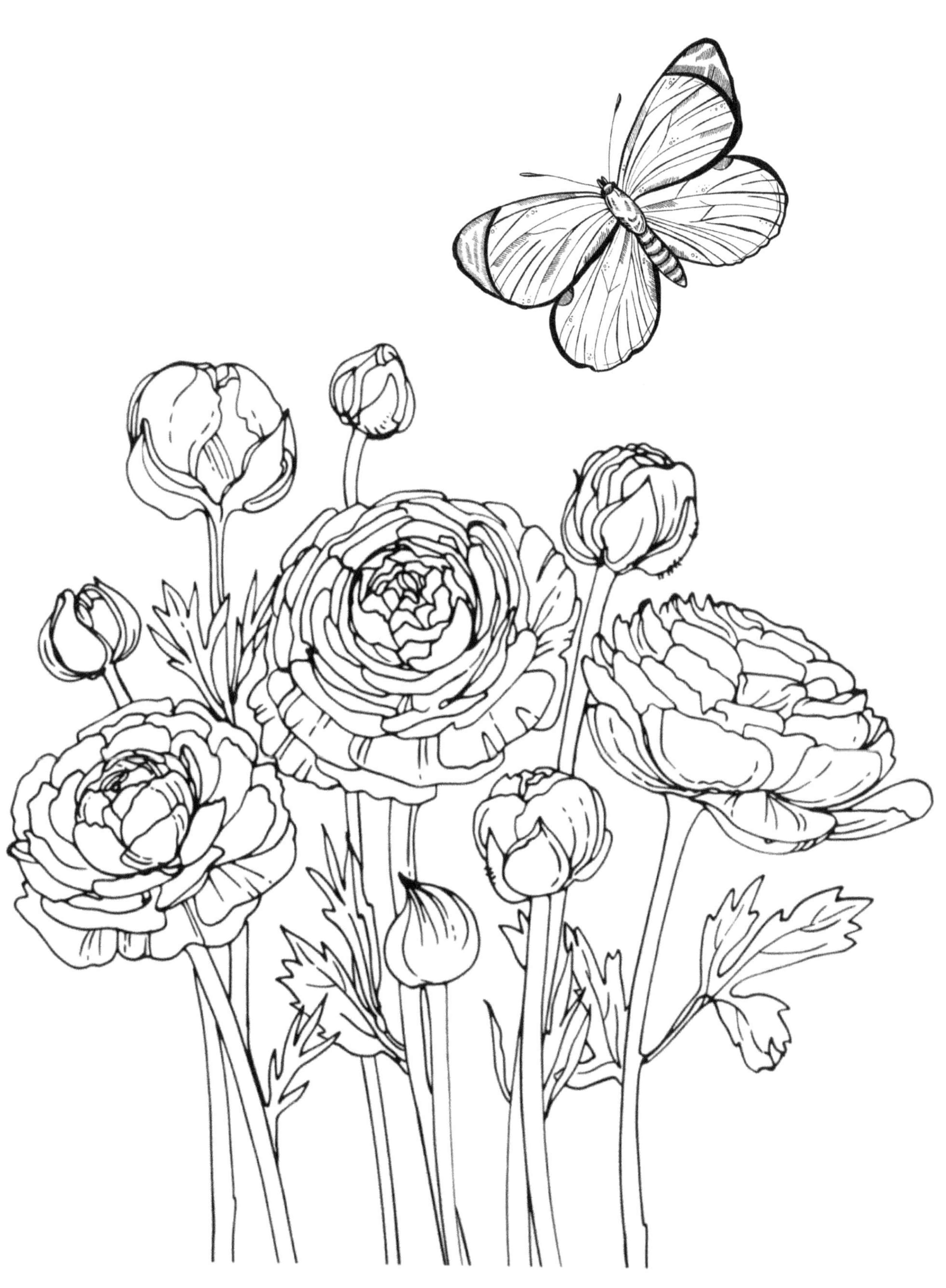